Utah's Green River

A Fly Fisher's Guide to the Flaming Gorge Tailwater

Dennis Breer

Frank **Amato**

PORTLAND

Dedicated to

Grace who helps me live the dream everyday,
My Grandad Edward Glatz who set the hook on me,
Doug Burton and Ed Engle for their invaluable help with this project.

Acknowledgments

I received assistance from Mark Vinson
of Utah State University's Aquatic Ecosystem Laboratory,
who is currently conducting additional aquatic invertebrate studies
on the Green River. He provided the most up-to-date information. Identification
and information on cicadas was provided to me by Dr. Richard Baumann and Dr. M.W. Nielson
from the Department of Zoology at Brigham Young University. "Many thanks" to everyone
for their invaluable contributions!

Cover Photos: Dennis Breer
All photos by author except where otherwise noted.
Maps and Illustrations by Dennis Breer
Book and Cover Design: Kathy Johnson
Printed in Hong Kong
Softbound ISBN: 1-57188-111-5
3 5 7 9 10 8 6 4

Table of Contents

U.S. Highway 191 passes over the 500-foot-high Flaming Gorge Dam.

The federal government community of Dutch John.

Petroglyphs from the area's earliest-known inhabitants, the Fremont Indians.

Foreword

*U*tah's Green River: A Fly Fisher's Guide to the Flaming Gorge Tailwater is a superb guide-book, to be sure, but it is a lot more. It is not only a guide book to a specific piece of water, as the title suggests, but more importantly also a guide book that puts the reader inside the mind of a highly skilled fishing guide.

As any good guide book should, it contains highly detailed directions on how to access the various sections of the Green River tailwater, gives the locations of suitable campsites, and provides an excellent word-picture of the river, its configuration and surroundings.

In this same vein, its chapters with regard to river flows, seasonal approaches, the various trout species and strains inhabiting the Green, and the hatching timetables of Green River aquatic and terrestrial insect species are equally superb. Just as one would expect from an angler's guide book to one of America's finest trout streams. Fishing guide and professional fly-tier Denny Breer does not disappoint the reader in his excellent rendering of these subjects.

What distinguishes this book, however, are the sections devoted to the skills of fishing from a drift boat and wade-fishing, and Breer's highly detailed and expertly crafted discussions of the fine and complex arts of nymph and dry-fly fishing.

Breer's step by step instructions on nymph fishing from drift boats using strike indicatored flies and presentation methods can be applied to virtually any North American river where it is possible to float-fish, including the equally famous San Juan River in New Mexico and the "blue-ribbon" waters throughout Montana, including the Madison, Missouri and Yellowstone rivers, all heavily fished from drift boats.

The book is also rich in innovative techniques, such as how to rig flies in tandem and using a small dry fly or nymph in tandem with a larger one, and in the fine details associated with float-fishing, such as the teamwork needed for dry fly float-fishing and etiquette that will avoid on-the-water conflicts with your companions and others when fishing from a drift boat.

Excellent fly tier that he is, Breer has also included tying instructions for certain specialty patterns exclusive to the Green River, including the "big, black bugs," like the cicadas that turn-on the feeding juices of the Green's sometimes persnickety trout when they hatch.

Anyone who studies this book on the Green should be able to catch trout there in good numbers. More importantly, absorbing the skills so finely detailed herein should enormously enhance their ability to catch trout on larger rivers throughout the U.S. and Canada.

Rex Gerlach,
Garden Grove, California

Introduction

*T*he Green River has held a fascination for me since I first fished here in 1975. I was awestruck by its overwhelming beauty and unbelievable fishery. Unlike many rivers I had fished, it also had a great diversity of river environs, which for me, added to its desirability. It was as if this river had all the special attributes that an ideal trout stream would contain. The deeper pools only added to its mystery, with so many beautiful trout exposed throughout the river, what might live there? Since those early days, I have spent many days trying to discover those secrets that river's such as the Green, only seem to give up to us when we are very patient or over time. With great humility, I have been taught much that I wish to share with the reader, though with excited anticipation, I look forward to continuing this education. In all, between fishing trips and the start of my Green River guiding in 1987, I have spent nearly 2,000 Green River days acquiring the information contained in *Utah's Green River: A Fly Fisher's Guide to the Flaming Gorge Tailwater.*

My motivations for writing this river guide are simple. Foremost, it is to provide a source of accurate detailed information and to document this river's many seasons and moods. Over the years, when doing slide shows or meeting someone who has fished the Green, they often describe the river differently than I see it. Whether their experiences were good or bad, they often struggled to understand the river as a whole, I acknowledge that any river can provide a number of different experiences, this river is no exception. However, most rivers also have their constants, reporting those are what this guide is about. Anglers need also to be aware, that there are many interests in the world that would happily deprive them of this great fishery resource. So, I also wish to nurture any additional interest anglers have in this river, this may help provide for the stewardship and protection it will need to remain one of the world's great fly fishing rivers. Finally, it is my wish, that by sharing what I have learned, you too will enjoy this wonderful river and its great fishery.

I wish to give special credit to some great fly fishing friends, many are responsible for some of the knowledge shared here. The list is long, but in particular I'd like to thank Don Puterbaugh for his friendship, early encouragement and willingness to share knowledge. Those who I have guided, all taught me something about fishing or about myself. The many friends who I have shared the river with all had their imprint on my life. Among these are those who encouraged and contributed to this non-writers efforts to produce this river guide are Rex Gerlach, Ed Engle, John Gierach and Doug Burton. Other friends include: Bob Marriott, Andre Puyans, Larry & Sam Walker, A.K. Best, Jim & Kelly Watt and Dave & Emily Whitlock. Last are the guides, both on this river and

Flaming Gorge Reservoir.

Watch for the "Drive Through the Ages" signs on U.S. Hwy. 191 that describe the geological periods through which you pass.

A great views of Flaming Gorge Reservoir en route to Manila, Utah.

others that have given so freely and willingly. This list is infinite, but I do wish to mention Wayne Dawson, Ben Munroe, Carl "Boomer" Stout, Mike Sergeant, Ed Emory, Emmett Heath, Larry Tullis, Larry Henderson and Allan Woolley. A special thanks to Neil Luehring, my friend and business partner.

Dennis Breer,
Dutch John, Utah

Welcome to Flaming Gorge Country

*T*he northeast corner of Utah is a region of rugged beauty, rich in geology and wildlife, and isolated from the population centers of the Inter-mountain West. This is a land steeped in history with rugged mountain men, adventurers, fur traders such as William Henry Ashley, the one-armed explorer Major John Wesley Powell with his famous expeditions, outlaw Butch Cassidy and his notorious Wild Bunch, and was once the wintering grounds for Ute and Shoshone Indian tribes. Though removed by more than one hundred years, residents still reflect their forefathers' adventuresome pioneer spirit and independence. Today, their lives are centered around traditional pursuits in ranching, farming, mining, timber and recreation.

This is an area of diverse terrain, a transition between the high Red Desert with its sagebrush, stands of juniper and pinion pine to the north, and the east-west ranging Uinta Mountains with their forests of aspen and lodgepole pine to the south. Provided within this realm is a complete ecosystem containing habitat for; big game animals, cougar, bighorn sheep, river otters, birds of prey, migratory waterfowl, upland game birds, and numerous other creatures. All of this exists within the sparsely populated 682 square miles of Daggett County, whose full-time resident population is only 700 people. Neither of its two principle cities, Manila or Dutch John, contain a single stoplight. At the heart of this expanse is the Flaming Gorge National Recreational Area featuring Flaming Gorge Reservoir, and its crowned jewel, the Green River. Annual visitation at this N.R.A. exceeds 1.5 million people who engage in outdoor activities such as boating, fishing, river running, water skiing, hiking, camping and hunting. This is "Flaming Gorge Country".

The Green River and Flaming Gorge Country can be reached by three major approaches. From the south U.S. Highway 191 heads north from Vernal, Utah. Vernal is well known as "Dinosaurland", home of the real Jurassic Park, the Dinosaur National Monument. As the highway begins its journey from Vernal over the Uinta Mountains, you begin the "Drive Through the Ages", an exhibit that tells the earth's geological history as you travel through it, and past a phosphate mine before entering Ashley National Forest. The 32-mile journey over the eastern end of the Uinta Mountains takes you through forests and open parks that present countless outdoor opportunities and is abundant in wildlife. On the north side of the mountains you will enter the Flaming Gorge National Recreational Area headquartered in Manila, Utah. Shortly thereafter, as the highway begins to descend the north slope, you will get the first real look at Flaming Gorge Country with its rock faces, deep gorges and breathtaking terrain. At this point you might come to realize what all of us who live in Flaming Gorge Country know, all roads here lead either uphill or downhill. In a short distance you reach the intersection of Highways 191 and Route 44 known as Greendale Junction.

Steering straight ahead to the west at Greendale Junction will put you on Route 44 which originates there, the sign says Salt Lake City 202 miles. Within four miles you will pass the turn off for the Red Canyon Visitors Complex and Red Canyon Lodge. Route 44 continues along the Uinta Mountains encountering inter-connecting roads accessing forested areas, high mountain lakes and

The snowcapped Uinta Mountains and the Flaming Gorge Reservoir. The Uintas are the longest east-west range of mountains in the lower forty-eight states.

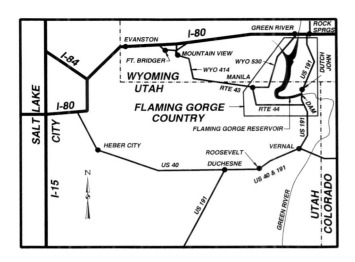

streams. During the 26-mile drive from Greendale Junction to Manila, Utah there are some great views of Flaming Gorge Reservoir as you descend the mountains. For a beautiful side trip, drive the Sheep Creek Canyon Loop with its tremendous rock formations and bighorn sheep. Route 44 ends at Manila, Utah when it junctions with Route 43. Traveling west on Route 43 will take you on to Salt Lake City, Utah. Going east on Route 43 accesses the western side of the reservoir and the city of Green River, Wyoming.

Traveling north from Greendale Junction on U.S. Highway 191 you will pass Flaming Gorge Lodge (two miles), several campgrounds and Cedar Springs Marina before reaching the Flaming Gorge Dam (six miles). The highway then passes over the 500-foot dam (elevation 6,048 feet) where the Flaming Gorge Reservoir ends its 91-mile run from its beginnings near Green River, Wyoming. Below the dam, the cold and clear Green River resumes the journey it started as a small stream in the headwaters of the Bridger Wilderness Area of Wyoming. Considering this river's overall length, Fontenelle and Flaming Gorge reservoirs are just brief intrusions in its quest to flow downstream several hundred miles and merge with the Colorado River. Three miles north of the dam is the community of Dutch John, Utah. This formerly government-owned village was "privatized" by Congress in 1998. Once the transfer of ownership is completed this 2400-acre townsite will be available for development of retail businesses and private homes. See Appendix "E" for the current local services available in Dutch John. One hundred yards north of Dutch John, a five-mile-long road originates, traveling east to Little Hole, the popular Green River access point.

Continuing north on U.S. Highway 191, you leave Flaming Gorge National Recreational Area and cross the Wyoming state line nine miles from Dutch John. Just over the state line is Minnie's Gap, where the Clay Basin Road travels east 19 miles to access the Browns Park portions of the Green River. This mostly gravel, partially paved road eventually connects with paved Colorado Highway 318 and provides a back road access to Browns Park from Maybell, Colorado. Travelers should note that Jesse Ewing Canyon on this road contains a steep gravelly 14 percent grade section during the descent into Browns Park. This road can be a mess when it rains. Future plans call for the possible paving and re-routing portions of this road. Allow a minimum of one hour for travel from Dutch John to Browns Park. By traveling 57 miles north from Minnie's Gap on U.S. Highway 191, you reach Interstate 80 a few miles west of Rock Springs, Wyoming. All major roads leading into Flaming Gorge Country are maintained. However, winter travelers should beware, some portions of U.S. Highway 191 north of the Wyoming state line can experience brief closures during winter due to snow drifts.

The physical beauty of Flaming Gorge Country.

The Green River Corridor

The Green River below the Flaming Gorge Dam has been divided into three distinct sections: A, B, and C. These designations were assigned to the river by the U.S. Forest Service for the purpose of management and are widely accepted by those familiar with the river. The physical terrain creates these natural divisions of the river and limits access points for each river section.

"A" Section-Red Canyon is approximately 7.2 miles from the Flaming Gorge Dam (Spillway) to Little Hole. "B" Section-Middle River starts at Little Hole and is approximately 9.0 miles in distance to the Indian Crossing boat ramp. "C" Section-Browns Park starts at Indian Crossing boat ramp and is approximately 11.0 miles in distance to the Swallow Canyon boat ramp. The remaining 2.0 miles to the Utah/Colorado state line receives light fishing and is really the end of the trout water within the "Flaming Gorge Tailwater." Some trout do exist below this point of the river but the habitat favors the warm water species most.

About Red Canyon

Red Canyon's rugged beauty reflects the millions of years in its genesis. Following the formation of the mountains, upthrusts and erosion shaped its future as the river somehow found its way down through the layers of rocks, formed billions of years ago in the Pre-Cambrian age. These are among the oldest rocks in North America. Red Canyon formed as the Green River flows cut simultaneously through several smaller canyons (Horseshoe, Kingfisher, Hideout) just southeast of what is now Manila, Utah. The original canyon in its pre-dam years must have been a wonder as it reached depths of 1600 feet and ran nearly thirty miles to its end at Little Hole. Today what remains intact of this once-great canyon is the seven miles on its eastern end. The rest was inundated by the waters of the Flaming Gorge Reservoir in 1963. Spectacular views of the old river channel may be viewed by visiting the scenic overlooks such as Red Canyon Visitor Center and Dowd Mountain overlook on the southern end of the reservoir.

"A" Section: Red Canyon

The Aquarium

The canyon walls surrounding the 500-foot Flaming Gorge Dam often exceed 800 feet in height, but descend to less than 400 feet just before Little Hole. The river drops nearly 75 feet and has nine named rapids in this 7.2 mile stretch. This beautiful river-filled canyon section is certainly this area's featured attraction. It receives ninety percent of the river's use due to its easy access and large trout population. It attracts many other users besides fishermen, especially recreational rafters in summer months.

River access and parking at the Spillway boat ramp. Note the steep trail from the parking lot to the boat ramp.

Anglers can access the river, boat ramp, and parking areas directly below the dam via the steep and winding Spillway road. This is a "Day Use Only Area" with no camping or fires allowed. The Little Hole Trail travels this entire stretch of river on its north side. It can be accessed at either the Spillway or at Little Hole. Both access points have ample parking areas and the trail heads are well marked. The boat ramps are managed by U.S. Forest Service from April to November. Some use fees may be charged in these areas.

Trout populations and habitat in this section are some of the healthiest in the world. Past population estimates by fisheries biologists have sometimes exceeded 20,000 catchable trout per mile. That is an incredible four trout per linear foot of river! Rainbow, brown and cutthroat trout seem to fill every riffle and pool. Even an occasional brook trout is found here. The river's large boulders, gravel bottoms, and crystal-clear water flowing over aquatic vegetation beds provides this trout population with an abundance of quality habitat. This habitat provides many places where trout gather to feed and are visibly exposed. They often occupy feeding stations in the riffles or tails of pools waiting for insects brought to them by the river's drift. Others can be seen milling around the large pools, gently sipping insects from the river's surface. The river's most active trout can even be observed rooting scuds and other small insects from the river's vegetation.

Between the crystal-clear water and visible trout, the "A" Section of the upper river deserves the name given to it by the river guides, "the aquarium". Few rivers offer the trout-viewing opportunities found here. In fact, it is often so good to the point of distraction. These trout are exposed to a lot of human activity and, consequently, many are not easily moved or spooked. So anglers can spend many hours watching trout interacting with their environment; I have learned much about their behavior doing exactly that.

Even with all of this visibility not all of the river's trout are visible, rarely will you see the truly trophy trout. Structured parts of the river do contain troughs and deep pools where many trout remain concealed and escape pressure from anglers.

The first four miles (Spillway boat ramp to Mile 4) of this canyon section resemble a large spring creek. It is characterized by long deep pools and glides with abundant structure and flowing aquatic weed beds. The largest pools were formed by rock slides from the canyon walls to the river bottom. These rock slides have pinched the river so that transitions between the pools are through heavy troughs or rapids.

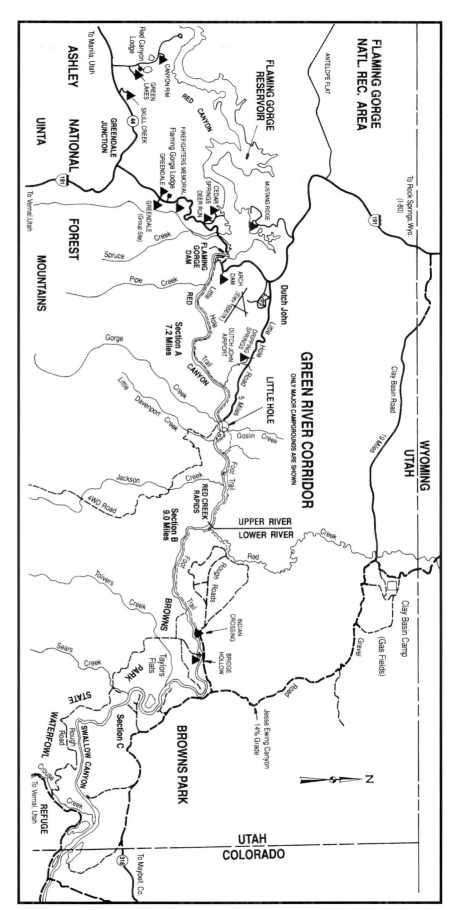

Between many pools there are flat water glides that average four to eight feet in depth. These depths restrict the water available to wade fishermen, but there are still many good fish accessible along the river banks, in the riffles, and smaller side pools. The larger pools average between four to thirty feet deep. Several pools in the river, such as parts of Merry-Go-Round, can exceed forty feet in depth. When light conditions permit, you can see into the greenish depths of these pools due to the river's exceptional water clarity.

The deepest of runs create the kind of protection that true trophy trout require to thrive. This river has an abundance of large and small back eddies (counter currents), more than any other river I know of. Back eddies provide extended fishing opportunities for the angler, by increasing feeding areas for trout within a smaller area. On larger pools, back eddies create such large counter currents, that it seems two side by side rivers, each running different directions, struggle to co-exist with each other. Boats are a definite advantage in pursuing the many trout that can be observed cruising and feeding on these flats and in accessing the deeper runs. While I personally view the Green River to be the "premier float-fishing river" in the West, walk-wading is an equally popular way for anglers to access and fish this river.

These first four miles are dominated by large

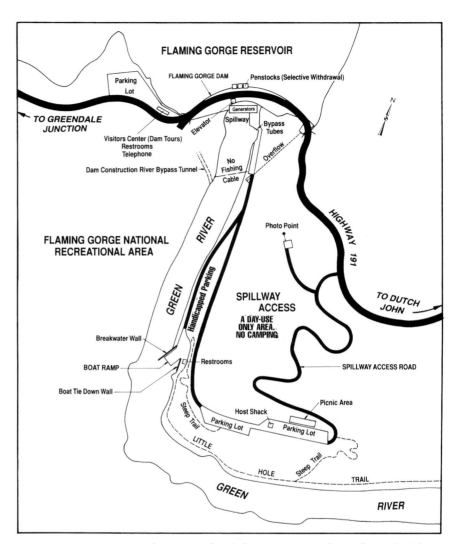

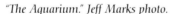

"The Aquarium." Jeff Marks photo.

populations of rainbow trout and cutthroat/rainbow hybrids we call "cuttbows." They average 15 to 18 inches in length, with a good number of larger rainbows and cuttbows that exceed twenty inches. The true trophy rainbows have reached 40 inches and weighed over twenty pounds. The Green River rainbow and cutthroat trout population are both heavily dependent on annual stocking, the natural reproduction that does occur is not adequate to sustain the fishery. However, many of the cuttbows are proof that some natural reproduction is indeed successful. Rainbow trout are most attractive to fisheries management because of their "catchability" (increasing angler success rates), excellent growth rates and their adaptability to this river.

There are two major cutthroat trout species available on the Green River. They have a wide river distribution, but their stronghold is in the slower river stretches and larger pools of Red Canyon. The Snake River cutthroat is recognizable by its many fine spots (almost freckled). The Yellowstone cutthroat is recognizable by its limited numbers of large spots and sometimes flashy fluorescent head and marking. An honorable mention goes to the small population of Colorado River cutthroat, whose markings are very similar to those of the Yellowstone cutthroat. It

Yellowstone cutthroat trout. Jeff Marks photo.

may require a fisheries biologist to determine which of the last two species a particular trout is. Most average 16 to 18 inches in length, with the river record being a large 31-inch Snake River cutthroat.

The next two miles (Mile 4 to Mile 6) contains faster, heavier, boulder-filled water with pools between runs. This section is known as the Rock Garden and contains four of the nine named rapids on the "A" Section. The excellent pocket water found here contains good populations of trout.

The river begins to widen one mile before Little Hole (Mile 6 to 7) as it is released from the confines of Red

Many rock faces can be found formed on the canyon walls. This is the Snoopy Rock, named for obvious reasons, it overviews the river stretch named for it, the Snoopy Rock Flats.

Canyon. With the river being able to sprawl, it becomes shallower and easier water to wade than the deeper, stronger water just upriver.

One tributary and one spring contribute to the Green River in Red Canyon. The tributary, Pipe Creek, is 1.1 miles below the dam on the river's south side. Dripping Springs enters the north side of the river about 1.4 miles above Little Hole. Both sources come out of very steep terrain and have no importance to anglers.

Visiting anglers on this river section will often encounter or view bald and golden eagles, osprey, families of the river otters, an occasional deer, elk, or moose.

Little Hole

In the language of the mountain men a "hole" is a low, open place amid the mountains. The Little Hole area got its name from the "Powell expeditions" as one of their original campsites. Access is via the five-mile-long paved Little Hole road originating at U.S. Highway 191 just north of Dutch John, Utah.

Drippings Springs Campground at Mile 3 of the Little Hole road is the river's closest regular campground and is normally the only one open all year. The Little Hole facility located on the river's north side consists of three large parking areas, three boat ramps, numerous picnic sites, handicap fishing access, and is managed by the U.S. Forest Service from April to November. This site is a "Day Use Only Area" with no overnight camping allowed. Due to the high traffic in this area, I recommend that when using the trail, walk a good distance before you start fishing. The further you walk the fewer people you will encounter. There are great places to fish, but the trout are very "educated" (many have Ph.D.s) due to the heavy angling pressure. Some area use fees may be charged at Little Hole.

Three small streams enter the Green River at Little Hole. On the north side is Goslin Creek, on the south side is Gorge and Little Davenport creeks. Gorge Creek is large enough to occasionally hold a few trout. There is a rough

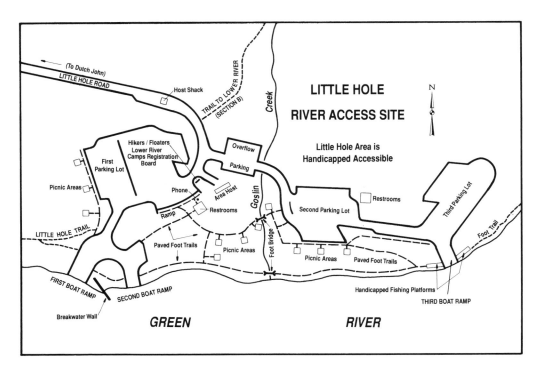

LITTLE HOLE
RIVER ACCESS SITE

Little Hole Area is
Handicapped Accessible

N

areas, non-existent in others. Just a one-third mile below Little Hole, a long bluff makes walking down-river near impossible, unless you are a mountain climber too. An easier trail to access down-river, bypasses this bluff altogether, leaving the main parking lot at Little Hole near the Forest Service check station. Once over the hill and down-river, the dominant trail is an unimproved fishermen's path on the north side of the river. In rockier areas it may be difficult to locate.

Visiting anglers should not let the attraction of Red Canyon blind them to the angling opportunities available. Trout-viewing in this river section still exists, but is often subdued when compared to the Aquarium qualities of up-river sections. This contrast sometimes leads to the false belief by many anglers that there are fewer trout here. In reality estimated trout populations are 8,000 to 14,000 trout per mile between Little Hole and Red Creek Rapid. This matches well with up-river trout populations. Below Red Creek Rapid, populations drop considerably due to major changes in habitat. Brown trout dominate the entire "B" Section, still numbers of all species exist. On average, these fish will genuinely exceed the up-river trout's size by one inch or more.

Brown trout in the Green River are the result of two initial stockings in l965 and 1967 totaling 38,000 fingerlings. They constitute this river's only wild,

four-wheel-drive road that accesses the south side of the river from Diamond Mountain. The Forest Service discourages its use and UDWR has restricted access for vehicles close to the river via a new fence. This road should never be traveled without the proper vehicle or in the wet seasons.

"B" Section: The Middle River

This section of the Green River is similar to the "A" Section in one way, access exists only on its extreme ends, and solely by foot or floating. The terrain here is distinguished by its laid-back hillsides interspersed with smaller sections of red canyon walls, the openness here allows the river to sprawl.

Trails in and out of this section are good in some

The Little Hole River Access Site. Note the Little Hole Trail that travels upstream to the spillway.

Trophy brown trout such as this 34-inch fish are caught annually. Scott Grange photo.

that the wild Green River brown trout starts showing up in larger numbers.

The first four miles of the river below Little Hole (Mile 7 to Mile 11) is characterized by interspersed large deep pools with back eddies, connected by broad, long, shallow- to medium-depth flats (three to six feet), similar to those around Little Hole. This area treats the wading angler better than the deeper runs of the "A" Section. Several areas of the river are channeled creating islands, Grasshopper Island above Red Creek Rapid and several others below. Wading is excellent for the first four miles, while floating is an advantage below Red Creek Rapid because of this river section's length, slower moving water, and wary bank-hugging brown trout.

Numerous walk/float-in improved campsites start one mile below Little Hole. There is a good mix of small campsites along with the larger group sites, all have fire pits, picnic tables, and bench seats. Camping is limited to these improved sites, they can fill quickly during the busy months. Downriver campers are required to register and pay for campsites at Little Hole before occupying them. These regulations also require all campers to pack-out what they take in, including trash and human waste. It would be prudent to check with the U.S. Forest Service on all the new requirements and what is needed for compliance before arriving on the river.

self-sustaining population of trout and average 18 to 20 inches in length. Truly monster trophy browns between 32 to 40 inches in length, weighing 14 to 20 pounds are caught annually. The river record is a 29 pound 12 ounce brown trout caught in 1996.

Green River brown trout are quality fish valued by experienced anglers for their selectivity, shyness, difficulty to catch, and ability to reach trophy sizes. These trout are strong, fight hard, love to jump (unlike some brown trout found elsewhere) and are in most anglers' eyes, truly the class of this fishery. It is in the runs just above the Rock Garden in the "A" Section

"Heavens Gates" just below Red Creek Rapids.

Grasshopper Island.

Red Creek continue until they decline a mile upstream from Indian Crossing. This is where you get that first view of the vast openness of Browns Park. Wading access to the river below Red Creek is best from the Indian Crossing campsites, via a decent trail on the north side of the river. The south side of the river is accessed from Taylor's Flats, it is a rougher, less defined approach than on the river's nouth side, but not impossible.

"C" Section: Browns Park

This thirteen-mile section of the Green River extends from the Indian Crossing boat ramp to the Colorado state line (Mile 16 to Mile 29). This historic area is disputably named Browns Park, after trapper and mountain man Baptistie Brown. The earliest residents to inhabit this area were wintering Indian tribes. Later it became the stomping grounds of mountain men, outlaws such as Butch Cassidy and the Wild Bunch, and a host of other colorful characters. This portion of the river and the land surrounding it, is administered by the Bureau of Land Management and includes the "John Jarvie State Historical Site". Jarvie established a general store on this Browns Park site in the 1800s.

The river valley floor is characterized by its big cottonwood trees, hillsides dotted with juniper and the open sagebrush lands of nearby ranches. The park also contains the Browns Park State Waterfowl Refuge that has several large waterfowl management impoundments adjacent to the river. Even with its openness, Browns Park does contain two canyon sections, Little Swallow Canyon

Jackson Creek flows into the Green River one-quarter mile below Grasshopper Island. Red Creek comes into the river four miles below Little Hole. It can create problems for anglers when it lives up to its name, it is a major source of a heavy red silt that clouds the river when it runs. These creeks are of no interest to anglers for fishing.

For the most determined anglers there is one approach to the middle of the "B" Section that requires traversing the back roads of Browns Park to a torturous trail that follows the Red Creek drainage to the river. This approach is possible but not recommended. This rugged one-mile-long trail, is not for the faint-hearted and depending on your actual approach, may involve some climbing.

The river's character below Red Creek Rapids (Mile 11 to Mile 16) changes from a gravelly, rocky bottom to a more sandy, siltier bottom that favors brown trout. Here, the river is shallower, flatter, slower, warmer, has fewer pools and fewer trout. This is a major habitat change that affects an angler's approach to fishing here. Later in this guide, the river will be divided into "Upper" and "Lower" River sections based on the differences in habitat created by Red Creek's silty deposits. The rugged hillsides below

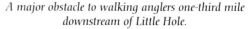

A major obstacle to walking anglers one-third mile downstream of Little Hole.

The "John Jarvie State Historical Site" was well known as a favorite hide-out for outlaw Butch Cassidy.

(False Canyon) and the larger Swallow Canyon. In Swallow Canyon, the steep canyon walls make walking very difficult, if not impossible. The best overall fishing access for this canyon is by floating.

The cable "restricted travel" swinging bridge in Colorado, just across the Utah/Colorado state lines.

The Browns Park road is the major thoroughfare for travelers visiting this area. With its connections to other gravel roads, it provides access to this portion of the Green River, even paralleling it in places. Smaller dirt roads down to the river are numerous, accessing many good fishing and primitive camping areas.

There are two improved Bureau of Land Management fee campsites here, one at Bridge Hollow and another at Indian Crossing (no electrical hookups at either). Many places along the river are suitable for launching or taking out boats allowing boaters to customize their floats. The last good boat ramp before the Colorado/Utah state line is Swallow Canyon, its marked two-mile access road can be found by driving easterly on the main Browns Park road. The next good boat ramp after Swallow Canyon is two miles down-river in Colorado at Swinging Bridge.

The "C" Section is the least used river section because of its remoteness, has less notoriety than its counterparts up-river, and does not deal well with a lot of angling pressure. The river here is slower, gentler, wider, and shallower in nature. Warmer water temperatures and fish migration can also effect angling opportunities here. Trout habitat is scattered, with some areas holding more trout than others. Anglers will have to search out the productive areas that contain good trout populations. Brown trout are the dominant species because of their ability to survive the heavy silt loads from Red Creek and the extremes in water temperature. However, there are a smattering of cutthroats, rainbows and cuttbows.

Outfitting for a Green River Trek

The recommendations made here for terminal tackle and other preparations, are Green River specific. Though other anglers may approach this river differently, my recommendations are based on the practical experiences of over twenty years on this river. Prepare the way you would for the Bighorn, San Juan, or other rivers with a tailwater environment.

Rods

The Green River is a large stream, indeed a full-blown river. Some river stretches provide spring creek type opportunities, others run deep and powerful. Rods that are effective under a variety of situations are the best choice. The river should be fished with, at minimum, rods of 8 to 8 1/2 feet in length. I prefer longer for my own fishing and consider 9-foot rods optimum, occasionally finding a 9 1/2-foot rod useful. These longer rod lengths give you the ability to cast distance (20- to 30-foot casts are average) with accuracy and the ability to properly mend the fly line.

Fly line weights are also important to your success on the Green River. Over the years a 5- or 6-weight line has been a real workhorse for my fishing. The 5-weight does a nice job because it does not bury your delicate smaller fly presentations, yet will still throw a weighted Woolly Bugger in a pinch. However, a 4-weight line can be fun to fish with when trout are rising to *Baetis* or midge adults on the surface. A 7-weight line is useful for fishing streamers or on a windy day.

Reels

Recommending reels is like recommending a car. They all do the same job at different prices and comfort levels. A simple recommendation: the reel should closely match the rod and line with which it is being used. The reel should be filled near its maximum, or at minimum with the 50-100 yards of backing that a large fish might require, but you are not going for bonefish. Some drag is also helpful, if only to keep line from backlashing on the spool.

Lines

A standard floating fly line will cover 98 percent of the situations you'll encounter on the Green River. Whether to use a Weight Forward (WF) or a Double Tapered (DT) fly line is a personal choice, I use both. For nymph fishing an ungreased Intermediate fly line serves well for most techniques where you may want the fly line to sink. A well-greased floating fly line, or one of the permanent floating fly lines now available on the

Wet wading is a favorite way to wade in the warmer months. Emmett Heath photo.

market, are ideal if you are dry-fly fishing or use floating strike indicators when nymphing. Sinking fly lines such as the Teeny series, or Hi-D sink tip fly lines are useful, but not necessary for streamer fishing if weighted streamers are used. For most nymphing situations sinking fly lines will keep you removing moss from the fly all day. I prefer using weighted flies over the use of heavy fly lines.

Leaders

For simplicity I prefer knotless 9- to 10-foot 4X to 5X leaders that can be altered by lengthening or shortening to suit my needs. Well designed knotted leaders are also effective, but I find them harder to alter. I prefer 9- to 10-foot 3X leaders for larger dry flies such as cicada patterns and other large attractors. In my experience, long leaders are the cause of much frustration, even for experienced anglers. A simple system that does the job means less time spent untangling, and more fishing time. Further details on how I alter leaders are given in later chapters.

Shock Devices

Want to reduce the number of fish broken off from setting the hook too hard? What about being able to reduce tippet size without compromising strength, especially when fishing small flies? Then you may wish to try one of the shock devices I have incorporated into some of my leaders over the past several seasons. For me they have reduced the number of fish broken off by 50 percent, saving lost fish, lost flies, and time spent re-rigging. They can be very helpful on the hook set when blindly fishing nymphs or handling a heavy fish that does something unexpected.

Several companies market these devices, one I use often is distributed by Phil Camera's Inter-Tac under the name of Bunjebutt. It is added to the fly line before the leader is tied on. A second is a pre-made leader with a shock section produced by Rio Recreational Products called the Shock Absorber. This shock material can be purchased separately on 25-foot spools under the name Trout Shock Gum. Whether you use these or a similar product, they are a great fly-fishing aid overlooked by many anglers.

Tippets

The two spools of tippet most often used in my box are 4X and 5X. Next is 3X tippet for fishing the largest flies from my fly box. Pattern selection and good presentations featuring drag-free drifts are priorities over tippet size when trout are selectively feeding. However, I will drop the tippet's size down to 6X when using the smallest of flies. The idea is not to handicap yourself by under-sizing tippets,

until you suspect the rejections trout give your fly are due to tippet size or its effects on the fly's drift.

Waders

The two main approaches to the Green River are walk-wading and float-fishing. Chest-high waders are a must for aggressive walk-waders. This river is deep and powerful and without them the water you fish will be severely restricted. Hip waders are suitable for non-aggressive anglers, satisfied to fish the shallower runs. Neoprene waders are a great choice during the winter and spring, when water and air temperatures are cooler. In summer when air temperatures may exceed 80 degrees, light-weight waders or even wading wet would be a better choice.

Some anglers choose to carry their waders in a pack when planning to hike any distance before fishing. They suit up after reaching the fishing area. Aggressive waders should consider using a wading staff. The bottom of the river is not generally slick in most places and is gravelly in nature. Cleats and studs are not necessary but felt wader soles give an added measure of safety.

Chest waders are appropriate for float-fishing during the cooler seasons and they serve as added protection from the elements. In summer they are a great way to slow cook. Light-weight chest waders that can be rolled down or, even better, hip waders are more appropriate during warmer seasons. Many anglers wear tennis shoes and shorts when they float the river from May to October. Water temperatures are commonly 54 to 56 degrees from June to October and wet wading is popular. Teva type river sandals and shorts are the choice attire of many river guides.

Clothing

Many first-time anglers visiting the Green River think they will be fishing in the desert. In reality the river (elevation 5601.60 feet at the Spillway) is located mostly within a mountainous environment. The air is dry which means that temperatures are high during the day and drop considerably at night. The dry air also means you will find relief from the heat in shady areas, the air temperatures are several degrees cooler there. The weather here is unpredictable. Some years are cool and wet, some dry and hot. I have seen it snow in July and rain in December. One person described the preparations for his trip, "as if he were going to the beach, but might go snow skiing too." Not a bad plan, especially for spring, late fall and winter fishing. No matter what time of year you visit the Green River, layer your clothing, and have adequate protection from the cold, sun and other elements.

AVERAGE SEASONAL TEMPERATURES (IN DEGREES)				
SEASON	SPRING	SUMMER	FALL	WINTER
MONTH	MAR-MAY	JUN-AUG	SEP-OCT	NOV-FEB
DAY	30-63	60-90	50-75	15-45
NIGHT	20-40	50-65	40-65	-20 to 20

Nymph Fishing the Green River

*E*very angler's approach to a fishing situation begins with their preferences. Preferences are more than what we do or do not like, very often they define us as anglers. Some are experts on nymph fishing, others see themselves as "purist" dry-fly fishers. The rest of us might like one approach or another better, but will do what it takes to ethically catch trout. It is my opinion that one of the special qualities of the Green River is its diversity in effective approaches. Ninety-five percent of the time you can do it your way.

This chapter will explore what some anglers consider the most productive approach to Green River, nymph fishing. Studies on trout feeding habits bear out the fact that aquatic invertebrates provide the bulk of a trout's diet. Scuds, aquatic worms, and immature aquatic insects (nymphs, pupae, and larvae) provide trout with opportunities to feed 365 days a year.

For Green River anglers this translates into year-round opportunities to catch trout. Indeed, nymphing is a very effective technique in a variety of seasons and river conditions. For most anglers, nymphs are used just prior to a hatch's emergence or during the long periods between hatches. On this river, nymphing is very popular in the colder months (November-March) when water temperatures are low and trout are less active. Many anglers will continue nymphing as a primary approach during the warmer seasons, or it can give way to a dry-fly fishing preference.

There are many systems of nymph fishing employed on the Green River. All work if they contain the key elements of good nymph fishing technique: presentation, drifting the fly in the "strike zone," detecting the strike, and proper fly selection. In my observations, anglers who are not successful on the Green River are either omitting or failing at one or more of these elements. So, accomplishing these keys when on the river is the challenge.

Presentation and Drifting the Fly in the Strike Zone

When wade nymph fishing, I like to make presentations to the trout from below their in-stream positions. From this approach I can work upstream and cover each pocket and lie. To set up a presentation I allow my nymph rigging to extend straight downstream. This is accomplished by first making a downstream roll cast. Then with a good pull off the water, I make one smooth accurate cast shooting the extra line needed to reach the target. This cast is commonly known as a "water haul" and eliminates needless false casting, which most nymph fishing rigs cannot do well without excessive tangles.

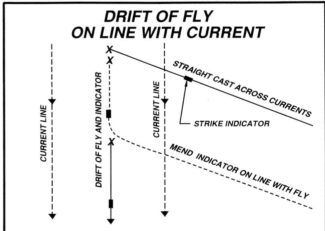

DRIFT OF FLY ON LINE WITH CURRENT

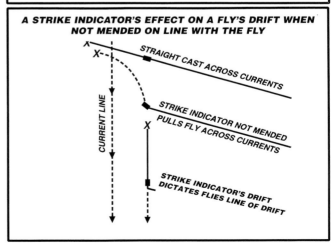

A STRIKE INDICATOR'S EFFECT ON A FLY'S DRIFT WHEN NOT MENDED ON LINE WITH THE FLY

A typical Green River brown trout.

Drifting the fly in the strike zone is an important aspect of presentation consisting of three objectives, proper drift lane, depth and naturalness. A straight upstream cast allows the fly to travel in line naturally with the current, directly into the trout's feeding lane. When the river's depth or nature does not allow a direct upstream approach, try an up-and-across cast approach. This cast requires actively mending the fly line to produce a good drift of the fly. It is important to realize that the strike indicator must be placed on the fly's desired line of drift. Failing to do this results in the fly being pulled across currents until it is following the same drift as the indicator. To counter this, the first mend should be to place the strike indicator and leader on line with the current line the fly lands in. This creates the desired line of drift for the fly, insuring that it travels naturally with the current line. Once that is achieved, making small upstream mends of the fly line above the strike indicator will take pressure off the fly as it drifts. This aids the fly in reaching the river's bottom and helps prevent the unnatural dragging of the line and fly across conflicting currents.

In certain fishing situations a downstream approach may be required. By stacking your mends, longer drifts become possible. After all casts, retrieve all excess line off the water. This enables you to set the hook and contributes to the dead-drift so necessary for productive nymph fishing.

During the drift, try to envision where the fly is. Then watch for any unusual movements of the line or indicator that would suggest a strike. Raise the rod tip sharply to set the hook at the end of each drift. This is for the strike not detected, or one produced by the rising fly at the end of the drift. It also brings the nymphing rig and fly off the bottom, making it easier to make the next cast. The whole process is then repeated.

Strike Detection

Proper nymphing technique and concentration are important elements to successful strike detection. Technically, it requires maintaining the correct correlation between fly, line, strike indicator, and angler. Strikes are seldom detected when the fly is allowed to drift downstream ahead of the indicator or fly line.

Anglers commonly mend the fly line to help the fly get down. The goal is to add slack to the system, allowing the fly to reach the river's bottom. Once this is accomplished, any excessive slack remaining must then be removed for strikes to be detected. Nymph fishing also requires intense concentration, too often anglers are unsuccessful because they are not focused. It is alright to "goof off", after all that is exactly why some of us fish. Just remember to stay focused when catching fish is of primary importance. Anglers routinely pass up the "tick" or smallest bump on the indicator. Trout are great at sampling the fly without your knowledge. They can suck-in, taste a fly,

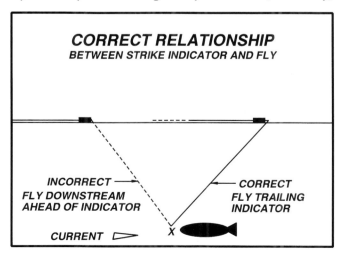

CORRECT RELATIONSHIP
BETWEEN STRIKE INDICATOR AND FLY

INCORRECT →
FLY DOWNSTREAM
AHEAD OF INDICATOR

← CORRECT
FLY TRAILING
INDICATOR

CURRENT ▷   X

and eject it faster than you can believe. It is my guess that only 30 percent of actual strikes are ever detected. Maybe less! When anglers comment to me that it was only bottom that moved their strike indicator, my response is "it should be the best hooked bottom you've ever had!"

Detecting strikes with or without visual indicators is not an intellectual process, but with time and experience becomes more intuitive. Successful nymph fishermen regard every unexplained movement of the line or indicator as a strike, then respond by quickly setting the hook.

Proper Fly Selection

Whether selecting nymphs, dry flies or streamers nothing replaces experience. If you have experience, you have your own favorite flies from which to choose. As a rule, when not sure where to start in selecting flies for any river, inquire in fly shops, guide services, or with other anglers having knowledge of the waters you wish to visit. Important questions are: what flies match the seasonal hatches during the time of your visit? what other locally favorite flies are effective? and is there literature available on fishing the area?

Of course nothing beats time spent on the river observing and experimenting. Once on the water, consider the other factors that will help you in fly selection. Are hatches present? are trout active or visually feeding? and what type of water are you fishing? Water type is important. For example, when dry-fly fishing on flat, smooth, slow water, patterns may need to be a more exacting imitation, while heavy or rough water requires flies capable of floating well.

A Typical Green River Nymphing Approach

The most common nymphing rig used for wade fishing this river involves using a long rod, floating fly line and an indicator. Rods used are commonly 9-foot-plus rods handling 5- to 6-weight fly lines. This river often requires that a long leader and the correct amount of weight be used to effectively indicator-fish its many deep runs. Leaders are often 10- to 15-foot 4X to 5X and have the large butt diameters needed to cast such a rig without hinges and tangles.

Weighting

Anglers need to adjust the amount of weight as needed for the river's current, speed, and depth. Normally, one BB shot or a weighted fly will suffice, but heavy water or high flows may require both along with additional weight.

Indicators

The size of indicator used must be large enough to support the amount of weight used. While the many styles of foam or cork indicators do this job well, in side by side usage, floating polypropylene yarn indicators seem to have a greater sensitivity to strikes and supports more weight. It goes completely under at the slightest pull, while others only produce an imperceptible movement of the indicator unless there is a solid strike. The disadvantage

Nymph fishing the Green River.

Beautiful, large Green River brown trout. Jeff Marks photo.

to using yarn comes when you are constantly adjusting its height on your leader. If caution is not used, yarn tends to fall apart in your hands when you move it.

The use of strike indicators is only effective when you keep them properly adjusted on the leader for the water you are fishing. When wading, this can be done by making several casts into the same run, observing whether the fly's are bouncing the river's bottom, then making adjustments until the correct depth is achieved. A common rule used to set the indicator's height on a leader is one to two times the water's depth. In faster heavier currents, the higher setting is needed to allow the fly to get down. However, for most Green River nymphing, my tendency is to set it several feet longer than the water's depth. This reduces the amount of slack leader that can develop between the fly and indicator, maintaining the ability to detect strikes. Failure to constantly adjust the indicator results in the fly being buoyed at an unproductive river depth. Anglers tend to ignore this factor, especially when fishing through a long run containing varying depths. This will result in fewer trout to the net.

Non-Floating Strike Indicators

Sometimes the overall depth of this river makes fishing with floating indicators difficult, if not impossible. When this obstacle presents itself, try using the "on line" type strike indicators, such as roll-on or sleeves that help in detecting strikes, but do not restrict the fly line or leader from penetrating deep water. At minimum, they provide a point of reference from which to look for strikes.

Approaching the River

Each run, pool, or riffle will require a different approach to fish it effectively. The best water to nymph-fish is where the river forms vertical shelves as it dumps into each pool. Trout collect in these areas to take advantage of plentiful feed and the break from the current. Additional places to watch for nymphing opportunities include reachable midstream boulders or any place that provides a break from the river's currents. While some river stretches lend themselves well to traditional wading, others present an extra challenge by requiring the angler to stay on or near the rivers banks because of water depth. Whatever your approach, remember to look for the fish before putting your feet in the water. Many Green River trout utilize the river's edges, providing extra fishing opportunities for the alert angler.

Some Fine Points

If you fish for long periods of time without a strike, make adjustments. Add more weight or adjust your indicator position, allowing the fly to get down even further. Not getting the fly down to the trout is the most common mistake made by anglers.

Under most nymphing situations on this river, you must deliver your fly to within inches of the river's bottom to be effective. Inexperienced anglers are those most apt to misjudge this river's depth because of its deceptively clear water. This results in improper rigging and less than desirable results.

Just as important, is to work for a good dead-drift of

Underwater rainbow trout. Utah Division of Wildlife Resources photo.

the fly, Green River trout are experts at detecting a poor drift. These trout are seldom leader or tippet shy when your selections reasonably match the fishing conditions. This is achieved when the leaders/tippet do not inhibit the fly's drift or the tippets are not greatly oversized for the fly matched to them. Most often, the trout are rejecting your fly or its drift rather than the tippet's size.

The last adjustment (not the first) is to change flies, especially if you have confidence in your current selection. Be sure the line-leader-indicator-weight-fly rigging is properly set up, then work at making a great presentation first! However, once a fly is given its proper opportunity, it may indeed be time to give another pattern a try.

Two-Fly Riggings

One way to double your fishing effectiveness is with a two-fly system. Many years ago, my friend and Green River guide Emmett Heath showed me how he trailers a second fly. This is done by tying a second tippet to the bend of the first fly's hook, then attaching a second fly to the tippet. This tandems the second fly behind the first resulting in fewer tangles than with the dropper method.

This trailer technique works equally well for nymph or dry-fly fishing. Depending on their use, tippets range from six to 36 inches in length, and 4X to 7X depending on fly size. The average length used is 10 to 18 inches.

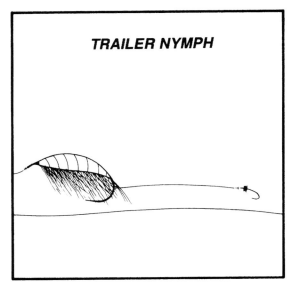

TRAILER NYMPH

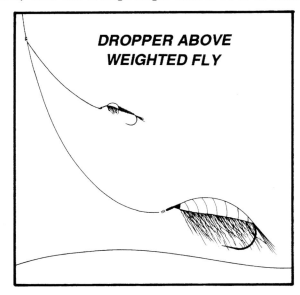

DROPPER ABOVE WEIGHTED FLY

With all multiple fly setups, make sure you are not violating a river's total number of hooks allowed for one rod. Only two hooks are allowed per rod under current regulations on the Green River.

Weighted Nymph and a Trailer

I use a weighted nymph when it is critical to fish the bottom, and to that I often add a trailer fly. The weighted fly is used first in lieu of split-shot, though sometimes an additional shot is needed. By using two flies, versus one fly and a shot, you effectively double your opportunity for a strike. In addition, the weighted nymph will sometimes act as an attractor for the smaller trailer fly. A good example be would be a small size Brassie trailed behind a larger orange scud. Trout are often enticed to move some distance from their feeding lane with this two-nymph technique. They see and investigate the larger fly, but may take the smaller fly instead. This adds additional effectiveness to your smaller fly that the fish might not otherwise have seen.

The only drawback to any two-nymph system is that when the rigging is broken off, two flies are lost!

Weighted Nymph and a Dropper

Just prior to a hatch's emergence, nymphs often swim slightly off the river's bottom. This results in the trout actively feeding on, even pursuing, these nymphs. During this period a smaller dropper fly above the weighted fly (instead of trailing) will at times be more effective. By doing this you flag the fly in the trout's face. Again, the larger fly can bring attention to the smaller one.

Suspending Nymphs

Trout respond to swimming or rising nymphs during a hatch with a noticeable increase in their activity. In slow water they adjust their feeding lanes to intercept nymphs in the river's drift. In fast water trout are visibly betrayed by their flashing, often darting in and out of the stronger currents as they chase down swimming nymphs. These trout are often observed suspended three to five feet below the surface, but you have to watch for them and watch their behavior. During this period a suspended nymph at the fish's level is deadly! Put the fly and a shot below an indicator and set the depth to the level of the active fish (three to five feet). You can also use the two-nymph system set below an indicator to accomplish the same effect.

Nymphs Near the Surface

When selective trout are actively feeding in the scum lines where small insects are trapped in the foam, floating or suspending midge larvae or pupae two to four inches down can produce strikes when all else fails. This is done by greasing a nymph to float in the film, or suspending it down a few inches with a micro-shot, below an indicator or large dry fly. Try substituting a micro-shot, with a sparsely tied midge pattern on a heavy wire hook, the hook itself will provide the weight needed to sink the fly. Small bead-head nymphs also work well for this purpose. When indicators are used in this situation, I prefer the roll or pinch-on floating types. Their small size and softness in landing near suspended, often spooky fish are a great advantage.

Dry Flies as Indicators

Large dry flies work well as substitutes for indicators. I prefer this two-fly (dry/nymph) method over the use of a standard indicator, especially in shallow water. Whenever a large dry fly is presented, it lands softer than a standard strike indicator, spooking fewer shallow-water trout. Trout are often attracted to both flies, moving to inspect the larger dry fly. When it is rejected, the trout may be tempted to take the smaller nymph if it is noticed. I do not recommend this method for fishing more than three feet down or when large amounts of weight are required. This usually defeats the ability of the dry fly to float. Again, small bead-head or sparsely tied nymphs on heavy wire hooks effectively sink below a dry fly without sinking it.

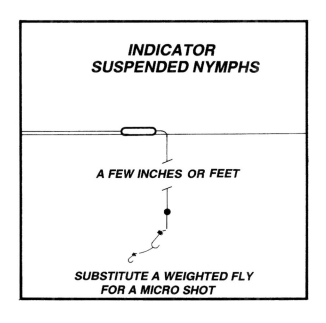

INDICATOR
SUSPENDED NYMPHS

A FEW INCHES OR FEET

SUBSTITUTE A WEIGHTED FLY
FOR A MICRO SHOT

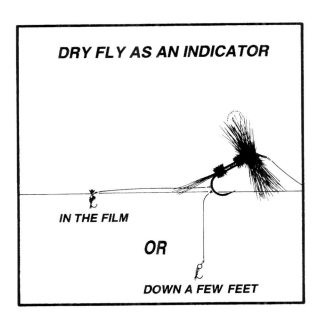

DRY FLY AS AN INDICATOR

IN THE FILM

OR

DOWN A FEW FEET

Dry-Fly Fishing the Green River

*I*t is the Green River's marvelous dry-fly fishing that has held me captive for so many seasons. It is my preference and I willingly admit my dry-fly addiction! What really excites me and many other anglers, is catching quality fish on large and unusual dry-fly patterns: Cicadas, Mormon Crickets, and Chernobyl Ants.

What is all the fuss about? Well, the Green River is a place where surface fishing these large and unusual flies has become commonplace! This is in stark contrast to many other tailwater fisheries that are known for the small-flies-only approach. What accounts for this difference? Most of the insects these flies imitate are large terrestrials. So along with the smaller aquatic insect hatches, a strong terrestrial presence adds spice to the dry-fly approach. If your dry fly experience parallels those of other Green River anglers, it just might be one of the greatest of your fly-fishing life.

Dry-Fly Rigs

My standard dry-fly rig consists of a 9-foot rod, 5-weight floating line and a 9-foot, 4X to 5X leader with ample butt sections that will easily turn over the fly. For smaller dries I add a 2-foot, 6X or smaller tippet section sized to match the fly.

Large dry flies such as Cicadas or Mormon Crickets require a 6- to 7 1/2-foot, 2X to 3X leaders. The goal here is to use the shortest leader/tippet combination possible that still casts the fly well without compromising good drifts. When it comes to dry-fly fishing, I believe simplicity is bliss!

Dry-Fly Presentation

The dry-fly fishing techniques used by most anglers will work on the Green River if they contain the key elements of a good dry-fly presentation that I like to call

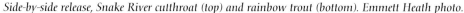

Side-by-side release, Snake River cutthroat (top) and rainbow trout (bottom). Emmett Heath photo.

Dry-fly fishing the large back-eddy in Mother-In-Law.

"line management." The first element is preparing your line, then making a smooth accurate presentation. This improves efficiency and avoids spooking fish. The second element is mending when necessary. This places the line in its proper position on the water to accomplish the drift desired. The last element is to retrieve all excess line. This reduces drag, ensures a dead-drift, improves the ability to set the hook and prepares you for the next cast.

Approaching the River

Wading anglers should fish traditional upstream dry-fly methods on the Green River. Quality trout occupy this river's edges, pools, large and small back eddies, flats, and fast water stretches. In all these areas, a well-placed dry fly may bring trout up to feed on the surface.

Fly pattern selection is often determined by the water types you fish. Flat, smooth water requires more exacting imitations, while fast or broken water needs flies that float well. Remember to look for trout that occupy the river's edges before putting your feet in the water! Many anglers make the mistake of standing where they should be fishing.

Boats give anglers an advantage in fishing those harder to reach lies. All river sections are open to the dry-fly approach.

Timing

From April to October the best time of day to dry-fly fish is generally around 9:00 to 10:00 a.m. into the early evening hours. Exceptions to this are the hatches of Tricos (early morning) and caddis (sometimes late evening).

In the warmer summer months, fish-catching is slowest in the heat of the day (2:00 to 4:00 p.m.). By fishing when the air begins to cool your catch rate will improve. However, one thing to watch for is the small midday increase in river flow that commonly occurs daily from July to October. If this occurs it provides cooler water and some terrestrials are caught in the river's drift, often stimulating the trout (especially browns) to feed even in the heat of the day.

Large, fluctuating river flows can severely impact dry-fly fishing, often making nymph fishing the more productive method. However, high, stable flows with the added stimulus of a hatch will provide excellent dry-fly opportunities.

From outstanding winter midge fishing to fishing terrestrials in summer, trout can be caught on the surface any day of the year. See "The Green River in Winter" chapter (page 51), for the season's (November to March) recommendations.

Hatches

As fly fishers, the accurate imitation of insects and proper fly presentation are important aspects of our sport. When hatches are present, match them! Watch the rise forms to determine which stage of the hatch trout are keying on.

Trout only partially break the surface with parts of their bodies (fins, backs, tails) while taking emergers. Their nose will protrude above the water's surface when taking insects from the surface.

During a hatch, it is best to work to an individual or small group of active trout by sight-fishing. Reasonable imitation and a good presentation (especially with a natural drift) will bring trout to your net.

Hatchless Periods

Many anglers believe that there has to be a hatch present to effectively fish dry flies. Not true! There are significant periods of time when hatches are not occurring on the Green yet trout can still be drawn to take a dry fly. Despite the lack of apparent surface activity by the insects or trout, you can experiment with dry flies anytime.

Terrestrials become a very important supplement in the trout's diet during these hatchless periods. Presenting their imitations is a very important part of dry-fly fishing the Green River because it is highly productive.

Similarly, attractor dry flies become very important as searching flies when nothing specific is happening. In fact, fishing with Green River terrestrial and attractor flies have produced more trout for me than any other approach. Often, I productively fish the river with these flies, only to be surrounded by anglers nymph fishing. Is this their preference, or are they just not aware of how susceptible Green River trout are to dry flies?

Selectivity

In the not-too-distant past, Green River trout were easier to catch. Not that they were pushovers, but it was not uncommon for anglers to have thirty- to fifty-fish days.

These catch rates still occur on the Green River, but not with the regularity they once did. What has changed? I believe that increasing pressure from skilled anglers, along with the increased practice of catch and release have affected changes in the fishing. The end result is increased selectivity which is not all that uncommon in tailwater trout. In his wonderful *Green River River Journal*, Larry Tullis made a strong case for this. I agree!

What can an angler do to combat these changes in trout with Ph.D.s in selectivity? Let us examine some possibilities.

Approaching the Trout

There is no substitute for a good approach and presentation. These trout may not openly exhibit any increase in wariness to a sloppy approach or cast by an angler, but after being caught several times they do learn what is going on. Even excessive noise from a boat will affect angling opportunities. It is as though the trout "tighten up" when being pressured. If you do not believe this happens, try being the third or fourth boat to have fished the same hundred-yard river stretch in a short period of time.

While anglers tend to underestimate their intellectual powers, trout can easily detect a phony drift and will reject an unnaturally floating fly. Success definitely improves when you approach quietly, taking care not to false cast over or line the trout and present your casts softly. Even better, make the approach from a distance, then make a long cast quietly and accurately.

Lunker Flats.

Successful fishing on the Catwalk Shoals. Jeff Marks photo.

Long Looks and Open Mouths

Make sure the trout actually eats the fly before you set the hook. Nowadays, Green River trout will closely inspect a fly, often following it, even pulling on its parts without ever committing to eating it. Other times they appear to have taken the fly, though never closing their mouths on it completely. Some trout may approach a fly multiple times before either rejecting or eating it. Be patient, wait until you are sure the trout has the fly and set the hook when the fish has started downward. This will increase the number of trout you will hook up.

Fly Selection

Trout soon bore of the same-old store-bought standards used by the average angler. Introduce new fly patterns or try different sizes of the old standbys. This gives you an advantage over other anglers fishing the same stretch of river. Smaller patterns often work well after periods of excessive pressure from anglers. The trout might feel it is safer to eat. Larger flies will often provoke a response when nothing else does, maybe they just give a different look.

Changing Silhouettes

Once you catch a trout on a fly, it's as though they spread the word about your fly. If you are not doing well and you are sure your technique is good, experiment by changing the fly's silhouette from a Wulff (upwing) to a Trude (downwing). This switch has worked well for me, often bringing otherwise stubborn trout to the net.

Leading the Trout

Always lead a hooked trout away from other feeding fish so as not to scare or stir the others up.

It takes hard work in all these areas to stay ahead of the trout. I rank new pattern development only slightly behind a well placed cast and natural drift. These trout may have Ph.D.s, but they are not infallible.

Dry-Fly Trailer

As with nymphs, I often use a large attractor dry to trailer a smaller dry fly. The advantage in this is that it allows you to fish the smaller, less visible fly more effectively by making the fly's location more obvious. Sometimes, only a small bulge or disturbance near the larger fly is noticed as the smaller one is taken. The larger fly serves as an indicator and goes under. A Trude and ant trailer combination is deadly! This tandeming of flies also doubles your chances to draw interest from selective trout.

TANDEM DRY FLIES

Nymph-Fishing from a Watercraft

*F*loat-fishing from a boat offers a great advantage to the angler fishing the Green River. This river's overall size and depth reduces, even eliminates, access to a large portion of the trout population. Float-fishing gives you the ability to fish the entire river by providing access to the many quality trout in the larger pools and deeper runs. Floating also offers additional advantages such as a way to travel from run to run and accessing either side of the river.

Nymph fishing from a boat is a very effective approach. The nymphing techniques and riggings discussed for wade fishing are also effective for floaters. There is one major difference between wade and float-fishing. When wade fishing, anglers make numerous casts into the same run to achieve one perfect drift that results in a caught fish. In float-fishing, it is making one extended drift over long distances, through and past numerous fish, to achieve the same result. The boat rower plays an important part in achieving this drift. To be effective the boat's speed will need to keep pace with the fly line/indicator to extend the fly's drift time while paralleling its drift to reduce drag.

Strike Indicator Techniques of Drift-Fishing

Several techniques of nymph fishing with a strike indicator are offered here to help float fishermen get their flies to the river's bottom and to detect strikes. The most commonly used technique is called the "outrigger"(beside the boat). This involves making your cast and fishing 90 degrees to the river. This allows you to fish edges and shallow waters while the boat has minimal effect on the

Drifting the river in a boat will give you access to many of the center river trout that are unaccessible to wading anglers.

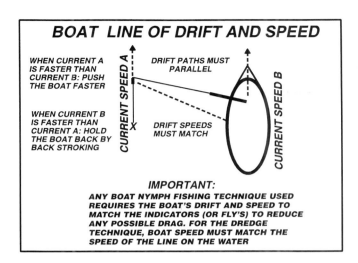

drift due to the relatively similar speeds of drift between boat and indicator. Proper mending will produce and extend good drifts. Take care not to fish excessive distances from the boat, this just makes it harder to control your fly's drift and to detect strikes.

The "down and across" ahead of the boat technique is also useful in drift-fishing. The fly is placed slightly to

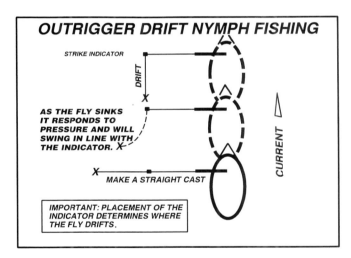

one side and well ahead of the drifting boat. This allows the fly to enter the water ahead of the indicator and rapidly sink without pressure on it. Once the indicator passes the fly, it starts the fly drifting when the leader is finally straightened. This technique is a dis-advantage when the indicator setting does not match the depth of the water fished. In shallow water, this technique may also result in the fly sinking directly to the river's bottom picking up debris or catching in the rocks. However, when correctly executed, this technique is deadly in medium to deep water.

Another Approach

When drift-fishing I often use the strike indicatorless, dead-drift, tight-line technique we have named the

Drifting the beautiful Green River.

"dredge" (trailing the angler's position). This technique starts with a standard nymphing rig consisting of a 9-foot-plus rod handling a 5-weight floating line with no strike indicator. Because the Green River is unusually deep when compared to many rivers, it became necessary to develop a technique that reached the many deep-water trout not available with ordinary methods. For this technique I have made some alterations to the standard nymphing rig to meet the needs of float-fishing anglers for this particular river.

To properly rig for this technique, the leader-fly line system must start with an ungreased fly line. By not greasing the fly line, it becomes an extension of the leader, in that it will sink too. This is the most important distinction between this and the other techniques discussed. The rigging (fly line and leader) is not buoyed (by a strike indicator) on the river's surface and is able to penetrate the depths required for the fly to reach the river's bottom. Warning: the modern high-floating fly lines that do not require dressing may resist this technique. Add to your fly line an altered, knotless, 9- to 10-foot 4X to 5X leader from which the heavy butt section is removed (average two feet) and the tippet extended to retain its length. Large monofilament and knots are not conducive to fast line sinking rates. Removing this portion of the leader aids in

the fly's penetration, even in the deepest runs. Though it is harder to cast, the leader can be replaced completely with several longer sections of small diameter monofilament.

This technique requires the correct relationship between the angler and the fly, it must be upstream (trailing) of the angler's position on the river. This is a short-line technique, using any more fly line than necessary is counter-productive. Start with one rod length of fly line plus leader, this is usually an adequate amount of line. Start the drift by making a cast diagonally upstream and away from the boat. Then, as the leader and fly line begins to sink, remove all the slack possible. The rod tip should be held steadily several feet above the water. Strikes will be detected only when a trailing, straightened, tight fly line and leader is maintained by the boat's matching drift line and speed. The boatman plays a critical part in whether this technique works or not. Mend the fly line straight or in line with the desired drift. Improper mending adds unwanted slack to the line. When there is slack in the fly line, or it is allowed to drift ahead of the angler's position (fishing downstream), it no longer maintains the tight line required to detect strikes and must be recasted. Strike detection is accomplished by watching the line between the rod tip and the water for even the slightest

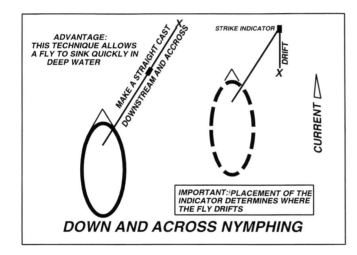

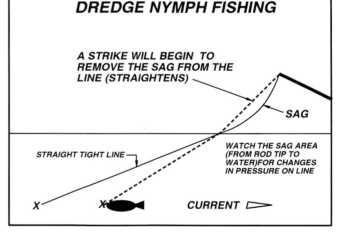

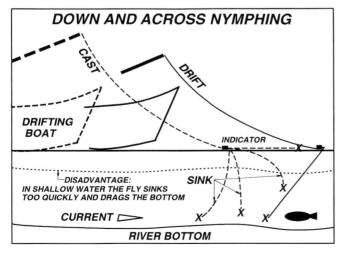

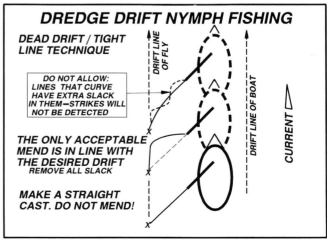

Many giant pools were formed from rock slides pinching of the river. This giant backeddy is Merry Go Round with Little Steamboat Rapid just ahead.

tightening or straightening. When the fly line and leader are straight, even the slightest change in pressure on the line is noticeable. Once you develop sensitivity to strikes, this technique is deadly!

The most common misconception about the technique is that a lot of weight is used, not so. The idea here is to get the fly down over distance by the long drift of a boat. However, using a weighted fly in addition to standard weighting setup can be helpful, especially in higher flows.

If strike indicators are used for this technique they need to be the "on line" types, such as sleeves, that help in fishing shallow water but do not restrict sinking in deep water. One angler I know paints the knots of his leader with fluorescent dyes. These aids help until the water being fished is deeper than the length of the leader, when they sink out of sight.

Some Fine Points

When float-fishing, there are several other fine points to consider. No matter which technique you use, fish a reasonable distance from the boat. Ten to twenty feet is optimal. Less distance is acceptable in the deepest runs where fish are not as likely to be influenced by the boat's encroachment. Long distances are counter-productive, as a long line lying across many conflicting currents

results in shorter drifts. It also requires excessive mending and more line that has to be picked up when setting the hook. Overall, there is considerably less control of the drift.

Another goal should be to reduce the number of casts, to work for the longest possible natural drift by properly mending. Drifts can also be extended by matching the fly's drift with the slowing down or speeding up of the boat.

Do not hesitate to fish the deeper runs. On many Green River sections there is a vertical trough that drops off four to eight feet or more next to the river's edge. Drift your flies on the deep side along the many rocks that define this trough for some great fishing. Also, watch those center of the river runs with great structure, they harbor some amazing trout. In these deep nymphing situations remember that it takes time for a fly to reach the river's bottom. Work to get your fly down and stay down. Each time you pull the fly up you reduce your productivity by removing it from the strike zone which will not be reached again until a considerable distance of river has been drifted.

Shallow nymphing along the river's edges and in its many eddies can be done from a boat by following the techniques and special riggings discussed in the "Nymph Fishing the Green River" chapter (page 18).

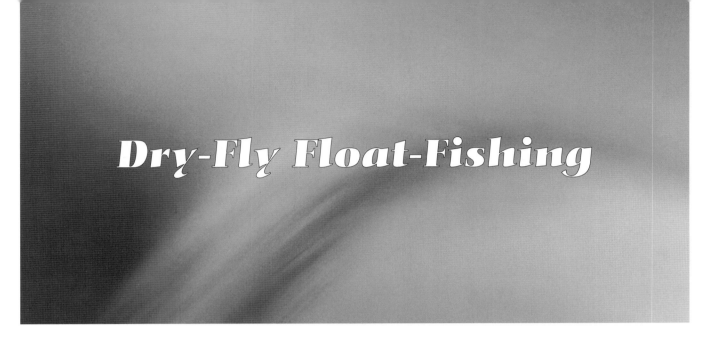

Dry-Fly Float-Fishing

*D*ry-fly float-fishing on any good river may be the ultimate experience in river fishing. On the Green River, the beauty of this approach is being able to place your dry fly on the river's edges, large pools and back eddies and watching them drift into a trout's awaiting mouth. This is not the cast-fest anglers often experience on rivers such as the Madison River, where it requires non-stop casting to effectively pick the pocket-water. Green River float-fishing consists of cruising, casting and extending drifts.

Float-fishermen also have the added advantage of reaching those trout unavailable to shore-bound anglers. Occasionally even reaching those large opportunistic fish that inhabit the most difficult lies. As with any river, the Green River requires time to gain the intimacy to find those areas that consistently produce trout. This river is blessed with a bounty of this type of water so if your favorite spot has an angler in it, try another. Look at it as an opportunity to explore the overlooked fishing areas.

No Poaching Please!

This approach to dry-fly fishing requires coordination and teamwork between the oarsman and anglers. The front

Dry-fly float-fishing allows a quiet approach to trout in difficult-to-wade river stretches.

angler's territory is from his position in the boat and (ahead) forward. He should never fish behind himself or face the rear of the boat; doing so results in losing upcoming opportunities, and limiting those of the rear angler. We call it "poaching". Once the fly is next to him on the water (just less than 90 degrees to the bank or boat), it needs to be picked up and casted forward. Fishing forward is in

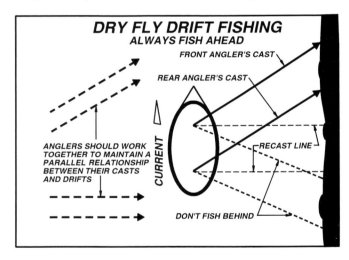

reference to the boat and does not always mean downstream. The advantages to fishing ahead are many: first opportunity at the fish, undetected approach to wary fish, longer drag-free floats, better vision of fish rising, and upcoming places to put the fly are just a few. There are few, if any, advantages to fishing dry flies behind the boat. However, anglers who violate this premise should at the very least cast and fish parallel with each other to reduce conflicts and tangles.

Rear Angler

The rear angler should also fish as far ahead as possible without interfering with the front angler. Any water that can be reached from that position is fair game. This angler also has the front angler in view, therefore it is his responsibility for the timing of casts. My preference is for one angler to cast, then the other, to reduce tangles. The successful rear angler improves his effectiveness when he observes where the front angler has fished, putting his fly into an area not covered. Because front anglers tend to favor the prominent lies, rear anglers often catch the largest trout when covering the least obvious lies. Large trout tend to move away from constant fishing pressure

Drifting the Fly

When dry-fly float-fishing this river's trout-laden edges, fish the most inside moving currents. Pinpointing this current is a judgment call that becomes easier with experience. Here's what to try for! Determine on which current closest to the river's edge the

One of the secrets to successful dry-fly float-fishing, fish ahead of the boat to trout that are unaware of your approach.

fly must be placed to allow it to drift uninhibited downstream. If the current line is produced by a rock or other structure, the fly should be placed right next to it. When fishing two anglers from a boat, I often try to get the front angler to place his fly a little out from the river's edge. Then, by having the rear angler fishing in as close to the river's edge as possible, we effectively "zone" the trout. With a boat, unimpeded backcasts and marvelous long, drag-free drifts are possible. Trout also inhabit all of this river's large pools and back eddies, they should be fished along the sides and next to the seam where the main river current meets the counter current.

Helpful Casts

High overhead casts are the most efficient, and are safer by placing the fly well above everyone on the boat. Side-arm and back-hand casts should be considered special approach casts and used sparingly only to reach those

The successful results of a prolonged drift of the dry fly.

difficult under-the-tree/rock spots. They are, at best, inaccurate and are considered unsafe as they keep the flies at the angler's level. Instead, learn to use the reach-mend cast, its use is indispensable for productive float-fishing. This is done by making a good over-the-head cast on line with your target. Once the cast is on its way, tip the rod towards the side of the desired drift. This mid-cast mend places the fly line and fly on line with the current simultaneously. It requires some practice, but when properly executed it produces the most beautiful, long, drag-free drifts of the fly. Once this diverse cast is added to your fishing arsenal, its use becomes an unconscious part of your fishing technique.

Long Drifts

The most common error that I observe other dry-fly float-fishing anglers committing is making cast, after cast, after cast. Where is the drift? Making multiple casts to place the fly on the ideal spot is known as "playing position." This results in the fly spending more time in the air than on the water. In fact, there are guide proverbs that addresses this issue: "there are not any fish up there" meaning in the air, or "you cannot catch fish unless your fly is on the water." I call it the "fifty-mile-an-hour trout" syndrome. A trout would have to travel fifty-miles-an-hour for one foot in order to have even the slightest chance of getting to the fly before it disappears. Making numerous rapid-fire casts that give trout little chance at the fly, most often results in spooking them. Nothing is more effective than a good cast and prolonged drift near the target, but once a fly has drag on it, recast, the drift is over!

A Resource

In this river guide I have tried to pass on as much useful drift-fishing knowledge as possible. However, *Drift Boat Fly Fishing* by Neale Streeks, has an enormous wealth of information for the boating angler. I highly recommend it!

A Green River Fly Fishing Calendar

This "Green River Fly Fishing Calendar" contains the important information that anglers need for a comprehensive look at this river. It should be consulted when making important decisions about the what, when, and where of this river. The calendar passes along the most detailed information by defining the river's nature with divisions. These divisions form this calendar's chapters, including: river sections defined by habitat, seasons, and river flows.

Habitat

First, I have divided the river into upper and lower sections which are defined by changes in habitat characteristics. The dividing line is Red Creek Rapids, 11 miles downstream from the Flaming Gorge Dam. The runs, deep pools, and large flats from the dam downstream to Red Creek Rapids all share the same rocky, gravelly bottom and habitat characteristics. Below Red Creek rapids the river is flatter and slower in nature. Silt deposits have built up along the banks and river bottom. It is a vastly different river here, needing to be understood unto itself. Since the largest percentage of angler use is in the upper river, its chapters contains the most detailed information of interest to the average visiting angler.

Float fishing.

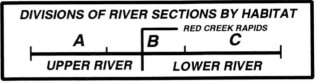

DIVISIONS OF RIVER SECTIONS BY HABITAT		
		RED CREEK RAPIDS
A	B	C
UPPER RIVER		LOWER RIVER

Seasons

The second division is by season. There are many different experiences and opportunities on a river that is open year-round. The seasonal information provided here is divided into segments titled Spring (March-May) and Summer/Fall (June-October) for each river section. Winter has its own chapter (page 51) "The Green River in Winter" (November-February). Within the seasons are references to

DIVISION BY SEASONS	
SPRING	MARCH-MAY
SUMMER/FALL	JUNE-OCTOBER
WINTER	NOVEMBER-FEBUARY

insects that are more thoroughly discussed within their own chapter the "Insects of the Green River" (page 60).

River Flows

The last division is river flows as released from Flaming Gorge Dam. The flows most commonly encountered by anglers range between 800 cfs (minimum flow) and 2800 cfs. The information given in the following chapters is

DIVISION BY RIVER WATER FLOWS	
FULL GEN.+BYPASS	8800 CFS
FULL GENERATION	4800 CFS
HIGH FLOW	2800 CFS
MINIMUM FLOW	800 CFS

based on these flows as a default. Flows of 2800-4700 cfs (4700 cfs is the maximum generation flow) should be considered as high flows. Because of their complexity, flows will be discussed in the "Green River Flows" chapter (page 52).

The Upper River

Spring

March

Spring on the Green River begins in March. In the preceding months, wintering trout tend to hold deep in slower water to conserve their energy. March's longer periods of sunlight and warming trends slowly stir the trout and increase their feeding though they will be found podded in these same slow runs and pools.

Even if there is the stimulus of a surface hatch, nymph fishing will remain the most effective technique to access the greatest numbers of trout. With water temperatures ranging from 39 to 44 degrees, they will not be willing to move very far for any offering. It is important to drift the fly on the river's bottom directly in their feeding lane. So to be effective, an angler's priority must be to actively search for the trout. In essence locate and sight-fish to the trout, do not approach blindly by fishing the water!

Many angler's assume incorrectly that trout always inhabit the same runs annually. Green River biologist, Steve Brayton, says that "wintering trout will often use different runs from year to year." So that great spot where you caught so many fish last spring will not necessarily be a producer on a return trip. I must emphasize, visually locate trout, then fish for them!

Scuds and Midges

Early season trout will take a variety of properly presented scuds and midge patterns. These invertebrates provide the bulk of trout food on most tailwater fisheries and remain important throughout the entire year. Scuds are fished effectively whether presented as a single fly or with a trailer to wherever trout are located on the river. Scuds for this season should be tied as attractors in regular and bead-head pattern styles. Larger sizes 10 to 16 should be tied in the bright colors of orange, pink, and tan. Smaller scuds that imitate the smaller *Hyalella* scud should be sizes 18 to 26 in gray to olive. Bead-head scuds have become very popular over the past few years, their effectiveness comes with their ability to penetrate deep water very quickly. For many seasons I experimented with different scenarios for weighting flies with some success. Even small jigs

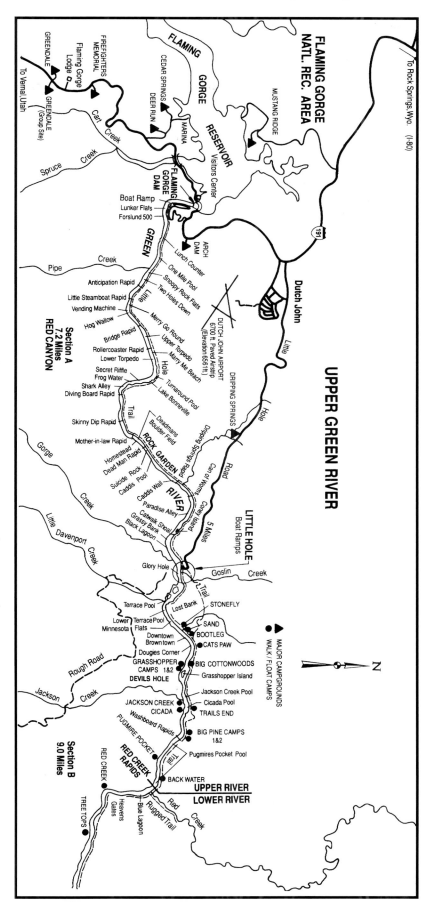

The "Selective Withdrawal Structures" attached to the penstocks provide controlled water temperatures through the dam to benefit aquatic invertebrates and trout.

work effectively in getting down in this river's depths, but many fly fishermen have snubbed their use. The recent trend of adding bead heads to many fly patterns has been very useful for anglers fishing this river.

An effective midge nymph pattern for any season is the Brassie in sizes 18 to 24 in the various colors of copper, red, and green. Of course you should try other midge larvae patterns as well. Adult midges emerge almost daily in the early season and can provide exceptional dry-fly fishing. Prolonged periods of warmer air temperatures and sunshine create the optimal opportunities for a good hatch. Midging trout are often only noticeable by their noses protruding through the river's surface, so you will have to watch for them.

Like their counterparts on the bottom of the river, midging trout will not move far to intercept a fly. Put the fly in their area softly and accurately, then allow it to drift to them. Simple, sparse adult midge patterns sizes 18 to 24, in gray, olive, tan, and black, are useful imitations. Green River midges only occasionally appear in the massive clumps found on other rivers. However, mating midge flies such as the Parachute Griffith's Gnat, Fuzzball, or Parachute Mating Midge in sizes 16 to 24, are productive patterns during most midge hatches.

Spring Baetis

The strongest *Baetis* mayfly hatches (Blue-Wing Olives) occur in spring. Though sporadic from late March through mid-April, they are strong from late April into late May during cold, wet springs. Large hatches are possible, but rarely occur on beautiful, sunny spring days. They prefer instead the cloudy, overcast, cool, even snowy days when only the most dedicated anglers are willing to venture to the river.

Duns generally start appearing mid-morning to mid-day, 10:00-2:00 p.m., with the nymphs being active for several hours prior. Size 18 to 20 *Baetis* nymph patterns such as the RS-II, Pheasant Tail, or WD40 tied in gray or olive, are effective emergers. Early in the hatch the most effective way of presenting them is by tandeming one to a weighted scud. Later they can be greased and fished in the film. Parachute Adams' and other low profile flies such as No Hackles, Compara-duns, and Sparkle Duns (C. Mathews) in olive or gray color in sizes 16 to 20, are among the most effective adult patterns. Trout rising to *Baetis* duns are very deliberate and have traditional rise forms.

The Earliest Caddis and Stones

The river's earliest caddis species, the snow sedge, comes out in February and March. This is a large cased caddis, and the blonde adult can be effectively imitated with a size 10 Goddard Caddis. They are very active during warmer winter days. Watch the streamside vegetation and snowbanks for their presence. Spring black stones also provide variety in the early season fishing with its emergence in late March and into April. You can match the nymph with a size 14 or 16 Prince Nymph, adults in the same size can be matched with a flying black ant or Rio Grande King Trude.

Early Terrestrials

The earliest terrestrials often start appearing as soon as the snow disappears. Though they are not very important to the angler. Yet, ants and beetles may start appearing as early as late March.

Spring Spawners

The spawning activity of rainbows in late March and April can draw big crowds. While I prefer to leave these trout to complete their natural urges, possibly adding some wild trout to the river's system, many anglers cannot resist them. Glo Bugs are the most commonly used fly to fish for these trout. I avoid these fish because they expend a great deal of energy in the spawning process, resulting in poor conditioning, and even mortality due to hooking and fighting stress. They often require little skill to catch and, once hooked, offer a listless, dogged fight. Besides, the large number of quality trout in the remaining non-spawning fishery far exceeds the few trout found on the spawning redds. You may work harder to catch them but the overall rewards are greater.

Selective Withdrawal Structures

The Flaming Gorge Dam has unique structures attached to its outlets (penstocks) that control river water temperatures. Prior to their installation, this massive 500-foot-tall dam released all its water from about the 200-foot depth level in the reservoir. The water in the reservoir chills at its lowest stratum to temperatures well below 40 degrees. These temperatures were not compatible with insect or fish growth when released from the dam year-round.

In a cooperative agreement between the Bureau of

The author with guests. A. M. Puyans photo.

Reclamation and Utah Division of Wildlife Resources, the "selective withdrawal structures" were attached to the outlets on the Flaming Gorge Dam during the winter of 1977. This simple five million dollar solution allows warmer water to be drawn through the gates of this structure at a selected level, effectively tracking the water temperatures within the reservoir. By the controlled raising and lowering of these gates (selective withdrawal), these structures seek to create ideal temperatures for invertebrate and trout growth.

They are visible when crossing the dam, you'll see the three boxes with large cable spools on top. As a result of their installation, the Flaming Gorge tailwater fishery lives up to its true potential as a world-class trout fishery.

The water in the reservoir typically starts warming in

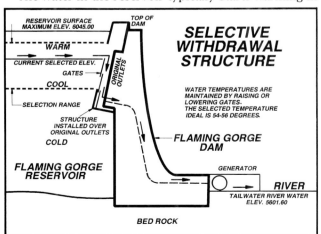

late March. The structures are opened in early April on a date requested by the biologists. River water temperatures through the winter average 39 to 42 degrees. Until water temperatures in the reservoir rise, opening the structures may or may not make a difference in river water temperatures. However, river biologist Steve Brayton believes that the trout respond to their opening in ways that are not fully understood. Even subtle changes in water composition, temperature, or an increase in nutrients may stimulate aquatic insects or trout. Trout respond to this stimulus by redistributing themselves, moving from their winter to more traditional habitats.

They also return to actively feeding. This repositioning and increase in feeding trout to the river's edges and pools is the most noticeable change resulting from the structures being open. When active trout move to the river's edges, it makes more of them available to wading anglers. In large pools and back-eddies, an increase in the number of feeding trout will greatly benefit floating anglers.

It is interesting to note that this water temperature change may be artificially produced by long periods of warm weather in February or March, inducing large midge hatches.

River water temperatures will climb throughout the early fishing season as the reservoir continues to warm. April's water temperatures will range between 44 to 48 degrees, May between 46 to 52 degrees. However, once obtainable through the dam, water temperatures are maintained at 54 to 56 degrees. The structures are closed in late season when water temperatures through these

At the river's low flows some mid-river stretches can be effectively waded.

structures can no longer exceed those available at the dam's normal outlet. This usually means warmer water temperatures than most rivers, even into mid-November.

Water Quality

River water quality can change in mid-March through late April when spring run-off starts, leaving many river tributaries running dirty. The main effect on the Green River is in staining it slightly. Even Cart Creek which dumps into the reservoir close to the dam can add to this stain by its direct flow to the dam's outlet. However, the river still remains very fishable throughout this run-off period.

The amount of snowpack in the mountains will determine the duration of this effect, but usually it lasts from three to six weeks. Except for this spring period, it takes a monumental storm or higher flows to effect the clear flows of the upper river. The techniques used for fishing the river during stained water do not change. However, it might be helpful to draw some attention to your flies. Try using the Tim Tollett "Flashback" style patterns to accomplish this. Useful Flashback patterns include the Pheasant Tail, WD40, Hare's Ear, and scuds.

April

April is what I call a 50/50 month, with half of the fishing done with nymphs, the other half with dry flies. This is a great time for fishing on the river because it may bring the first consistent dry-fly fishing of the season. Days with good midge and *Baetis* hatches are normally preceded by several hours of highly productive nymph fishing. However, sometimes entire days are still spent nymph fishing with scuds, midge larvae and pupae, and other nymphs when conditions do not favor surface hatches. So the 50/50 statement is more about possibilities than anything.

The last week of April is traditionally when the Utah Division of Wildlife Resources conducts its annual spring electroshocking and stocking programs. Shocking is done during the late evening and night hours when there are higher river flows to float their shocking boat. Commonly they will shock below the dam one night, then at Little Hole the following night.

Stocking usually takes half a day with the water being raised mid-morning. This flow generally is around 3000 cfs to enable the stocking raft to negotiate the river. The trout are planted and the flows are reduced back to normal by early afternoon. In the future, higher spring flows may alter the stocking dates. River biologists have been studying whether stocking is more or less successful before, during, or after high flows. Preliminary results suggest that later is better. Since the stocking of smaller trout is of great interest to larger trout, it does not hurt to ask the biologists for their agenda. Some of the real monsters on this river are caught during this activity.

May

May is also what I would classify as a 50/50 month. Under normal river flow conditions it favors dry-fly fishing. River temperatures continue to rise as the reservoir water warms, resulting in the trout becoming increasingly active.

Terrestrials begin to reveal their presence when the daytime temperatures average in the 60s to low 70s. Grasshoppers, beetles, ants, crickets and cicadas are all active in May. Their addition to the food chain is most important to a dry-fly fisherman. Annually, 70 percent of my non-hatch-matching, dry-fly fishing is done with imitations of these insects. The other 30 percent consists of attractor dry flies.

To be effective, smaller terrestrials such as ants and beetles should be fished next to the river's edge, the closer to the edge, the better! The Green River has become well-known for its cicada hatches and the resulting large dry-fly madness that accompanies it. These large terrestrials commonly start to appear around the first two weeks of May each year. Some years the hatches are stronger than others, so it will pay to do some local inquiries before traveling just to fish this hatch.

With Flaming Gorge Dam being operated each year for the recovery of rare native fish, high river flows during this month are a reality as the U.S. Fish and Wildlife Service tries to mimic the traditional spring flows. Reading the "Green River Flows" chapter (page 52) is a must for any angler planning a May/June visit to the Green River. This time period may always be fished successfully with nymphs and streamers. Surface fishing may be possible if there is the stimulus of an aquatic hatch, such as *Baetis* or major terrestrials like cicadas. This has occurred during several recent springs with some excellent top-water fishing even with the higher flows.

Streamer Fishing

Streamer fishing is an important approach to this river's more aggressive trout any time of year. Some streamers are taken immediately when they hit the water, others are preceded by extended follows. One useful approach is to strip the streamer fast in slow water, slow in faster water.

In slower water, you need to work the streamer faster so that attracted trout cannot scrutinize it. You need to cast it and start it moving quickly. In fast or heavy water, try not to retrieve it back too fast. Give the streamer time, even dead-drift it out of the pocket then strip it slowly. The heavier currents will contribute to a portion of the streamer's movement.

In winter, when the water is cold and trout sluggish, dead-drifting streamers are sometimes the only way to obtain strikes. Smaller streamers work well in the slower water. High flows, faster water, and following fish-stocking activity require larger or tandem streamers. Larger trout in this river are definitely cannibalistic, they aggressively prey on smaller trout, minnows, and sculpins. Woolly Buggers sizes 2 to 8 in a variety of colors are very effective. An important point to remember is, if the trout do not respond well to the streamer approach, try something else! The trout are either aggressive or not, retry later in the day as sudden changes in mood do occur.

Some Fine Points

In the early season the "A" Section of the river has the advantage of higher trout densities. However, the "B" Section has good populations of slightly larger trout. Rainbow trout will actively feed throughout the day, while brown trout operate more like a switch, turning on, turning off, during portions of each day. In the early season, the "turn on" occurs most often from mid-afternoon into evening.

Early Season Visitors

Spring fishing on the Green River is not much different from other tailwater rivers that have controlled water releases. Tailwaters often attract the majority of anglers suffering from "cabin fever," especially on three-day weekends and weekends with projected good weather. Expect anglers to fish when they can this time of year, but especially on Fridays and Saturdays.

The disadvantage to the "A" Section is that it will receive the lion's share of this use, but do not let this discourage you. This river's size alone makes it hard for people to dominate areas. Besides, with the high trout populations available here, you need only a very small river stretch to get the same opportunities found in most waters.

A common mistake made by most wading anglers is not walking far enough away from the upper river's only two access points. Remember that all anglers have to enter the river corridor at one area or another. What is important is not how many anglers there are, but what you do to separate yourself from them. Often trout in the access areas see far more pressure because of their visibility. If you are willing to hike a reasonable distance from these entry points you will find fewer people, plenty of water, and friendlier fish.

Floating the river is also a great way to reach the less crowded fishing areas. Additional relief from fishing pressure can be found in the productive areas below Little Hole. With a little effort you can hike down-river to other areas which also produce great fishing. Fishing productivity there can rival the opportunities in the "A" Section.

Bring Your Neoprenes

Weather in March and April is often wet and snowy bringing heavy moisture to the area. May will often bring rain as air temperatures continue to climb. This is not the time to leave your neoprene waders or cold weather gear at home. However, there are many blue sky sunshine days between the weather fronts that make for very pleasant fishing.

A Warning

A final note: Late April and May is the time of year when plants start blooming. Be aware that poison ivy exists in some places along the Green River. The U.S. Forest Service does make an attempt at eradicating this plant, but do not take this for granted. It is identifiable by the three glossy green leaflets. It is commonly on a vine and found in shady areas. In fall its leaves turn bright red as do many other non-toxic oak-type plants which leads to confusion in identifying these plants. Please be alert!

Upper River

Spring Fly Patterns

Scuds: 10 to 14; tan, pink or orange; bead-heads or weighted for boat fishing (used as attractors)

Smaller Scuds: 18 to 24; olive or gray (imitations)

Midges: 18 to 24; Kaufmann's Chironomid Emerger; WD40, red; Black Midge Larva, red or green; Biot Midges, olive or red; Brassie, copper, red or green; Parachute Griffith's Gnat; Fuzzball; Parachute Mating Midge; midge adults, tan, gray, black or olive

Baetis: 16 to 20; Pheasant Tail; WD40, olive or gray; RSII, gray or olive; Flashback versions of the above flies; Parachute Adams; Compara-dun, gray or olive; Sparkle Duns, gray or olive; Parachute Blue-wing Olive

Cranefly Larvae: 6 to 10

Streamers: 4 to 12; Woolly Buggers in all the usual colors; also try ginger, brown, white; crystal chenille bodies are also effective.

Spring Terrestrials: (mid-April to May) Flying Ant, 14 to 16; ants, 14 to 18; beetles, 14 to 16; (May) hoppers, 10 to 14; cicadas, 8 to 10

Others: Hare's Ear, 14 to 18; Prince Nymph, 14 to 16; San Juan Worm, 10 to 14; Royal Wulffs/Trudes, 14 to 18; Rio Grande King Trudes, 14; Crystal Trudes, 14; Elk Hair Caddis, olive, 14 to 16; Goddard Caddis, 10 to 14

Upper River
Summer/Fall

I have picked June as the line between spring and summer for several reasons. First, the river system is in full force. Water released from the dam will be in the 50 degree range and trout are actively feeding on a variety of food sources. Second, it is the dividing line between angler use of the river in spring and the multiple river uses found with summer. Finally, the weather is generally so good that Teva sandals or tennis shoes and shorts are considered appropriate fishing attire. Daytime high temperatures in June average around 70 to 80 degrees. Fall was combined with summer in this chapter because they offer similar fishing.

Summer Nymph Fishing

While the summer months are a very special time for the dry-fly approach, nymph fishing will continue to produce many Green River trout. During warmer periods of a long summer day, nymphs may prove to be a most effective way to move trout. Though they can be fished deep, try them first as a dropper from a large dry fly on the river's edges and shallower waters. Except for the specific match-the-hatch patterns, the nymph patterns of spring will continue their effectiveness. Remember to think midges and scuds! Whether it is because of a molting color stage or any other reason, scud patterns for summer can also be tied in orangish amber.

June

With the cooler months behind, it's time for the flies of summer. Along with an array of hatch-matchers and terrestrials, attractor patterns will also become prominent. I cannot stress enough the importance of terrestrials in the diet of Green River trout. Ants, beetles, crickets, hoppers, caterpillars, are all summertime fare to trout. They help fill the dietary void created by the lack of aquatic hatches during the summer months.

Summer hoppers will be larger, more abundant, and found in more variety than those in the springtime. Hopper patterns should range from the traditional like a Joe's, Whitlock's, or Parachute Hopper, to more suggestive patterns such as Stimulators or large Double Humpys. Anglers should also watch for those mega-terrestrials— the cicada and Mormon cricket. Their appearance (along the river corridor) in late spring or early summer will definitely effect angling opportunities.

Though the smaller terrestrial patterns can be fished by themselves, they are doubly effective when fished as trailers with other larger terrestrials or attractor flies. On good cicada years, their patterns can often be used as attractors long after the hatch is gone.

In summer break out your attractor dry flies. It is hard for trout to turn down large, mouth-watering offerings such as Royal Wulffs. Large, black, and shiny flies are also very effective. Patterns in this category include Chernobyl Ants, Crystal Cripplers and Crystal Trudes. Other large temptations include, Royal Stimulators, Double Uglys, and Royal or Yellow Humpys.

Late June will find mid-season hatches of Pale Morning Duns. These occur most heavily on dark, cloudy summer days. The nymph can be effectively matched with a Pheasant Tail. Adults can be matched with low-profile patterns such as parachutes, Compara-duns, and Sparkle Duns (Mathews) pale yellow in color.

The strongest hatches occur just below Little Hole and are present all the way to Swallow Canyon in the "C" Section. Caddis also have some presence along the river in summer, especially towards evening. Though you can match the caddis species that is hatching, I like using them as searching or attractor patterns even more.

People will always accumulate at the river's few access points.
Large groups of recreational rafters in summer will often crowd the Spillway boat ramp
between 9:00-11:00 a.m. Within several hours, this facility will have few if any people launching.

Recreational rafters have a great time yelling and having water fights. Though not aesthetically pleasing and often viewed as rude to anglers involved in their own activity, these rafters rarely impact the trout or the fishing for more than a short period of time. Anglers will need to exercise great patience when encountering the least savvy of these "other river users."

Summer Stones

The Green River has never been a river known for a great stonefly hatch. However, though limited in number and distribution, medium brown stones (goldens) will be found mid-June in some areas of the river. Watch for them in the boulder-filled rapids such as Washboard Rapids and down river.

Blooming Weed Beds

In July, weed beds can take over some portions of the river closing the rocky edges and areas where the sand-sharks frequent (sand-sharks are those hard-to-catch trout that lay on the river's sandy edges, feeding on midges and aquatic worms that are abundant in the silty soil). Watch for the new prime lies created on the weed bed edges after other areas are closed off.

Lazy Days of Summer

July and August are similar in both weather and fishing. This is the hottest time of year, with air temperatures averaging in the 80s. Welcomed afternoon thundershowers do occur, cooling things down a bit. These same storms can do their damage to Red Creek though, blowing it out more than any other time of the year.

In extremely hot weather, the most productive times to fish are early and late in the cooler portions of the day. As with most western rivers, the Green has its share of windy days. Usually these winds occur in the late afternoon as a cooling rain storm approaches.

The Bugs of Summer

Summer months are prime for caddis, grasshoppers, adult craneflies and damselflies. It is the best time for many evening hatches such as caddis. A size 12 to 14 Goddard or Elk Hair Caddis is deadly at dusk, besides they are vir-tually unsinkable and that helps in the waning light. After dark, try a black Woolly Bugger stripped across the top foot of the river's surface.

The pre-dawn hours on the Green River have never been exceptional for me, though some monster trout are caught then. In the early light of morning there is an increase in activity as trout feed on Hyalella scuds in the shallow areas and rocks next to the river's edge. Trout engaged in this activity will almost crawl in the rocks to feed on these scuds. Sometimes you only see their exposed tails and fins in the shallow water's surface next to the rocks. Anglers often spook these riverside-hugging trout when they walk along the river trails early in the morning. However, an aware angler with a cautious approach and presentation can catch some of these trout. Indeed, many have been caught on a well-placed small ant or beetle. The most productive surface fishing often is preceded by several hours of strong sunlight.

Tricos

In late August and into October, the cooler air temperatures encourage *Tricos* to appear around Little Hole and down-river. They will only occasionally be found up-river. This is not a major Green River hatch, but it occurs often enough to be mentioned. For anglers, the most important stage of this insect is its "spinner fall," which is generally over by 11:00 a.m. This stage of the hatch is well matched with a size 18 to 22 Black and White Spinner.

September

September is considered by many to be one of the most ideal months to fish the Green River. Weather conditions are at their best with air temperatures averaging 70 to 75 degrees. Many days are the blue sky and sunshine days that make fishing so very pleasurable. These cooler days

Floating congestion is often a result of groups of boaters trying to float together, blocking portions of the river. These float-fishermen are slow to realize that by not spreading out the fishing pressure they diminish the angling opportunities for everyone.

are a relief from the warmer days of summer. It is the commencement of autumn, bringing on the changes to the foliage, creating a visual delight on the nearby mountains!

In the weeks following Labor Day, the pressure on the river lessens with the termination of summer vacations. The trout are in their prime condition, fattened from all the insects of summer. It is also the return of the cooler-season hatches, fall *Baetis* and midges. As in spring, the strongest hatches of these insects occur on cooler, cloudy days. The *Baetis* nymphs and duns will be smaller than in spring, averaging size 20 to 22. Caddis will remain active throughout all of September.

October

The fishing in October is highly underrated. It is every bit as good as any other month of the year. Why people turn their attention away from fishing the river when the fishing is so good is hard to understand. For many, it is the beginning of the big-game hunting season, this accounts for some distraction. But for die-hard anglers this is prime time, with fewer anglers on the river.

October means "Indian summer." Beautiful weather mixed with the first cold fronts of fall require being prepared for all possibilities, even snow. Brown trout are starting to gather for their spawning time. Though hatches decrease, midges, caddis, attractors, terrestrials, nymphs, and streamers produce trout until the snow flies.

Understanding the Dynamics of People

Often, I hear complaints about western waters being crowded. The Green River has gotten a lot of bad press for being extremely crowded. In my opinion, this is a bad rap. The size of this river makes it nearly impossible for any one individual to dominate a portion of it. Sure it is common for other people to be around, however, this river is no worse than any other public waterway that has multiple use.

Summer fishing means that, unlike in spring where most of the other people around you are fishermen, you will have to share the river with recreational boaters and rafters. Webster's Dictionary defines crowded as: "a large number of persons gathered together." This does occur at both access points to the upper river, Spillway and Little Hole. The physical terrain surrounding this region of the river forces people to these areas.

For wading anglers the issue of crowding comes down to how well people disperse after they enter these areas. This can be a serious problem at Little Hole, where many people seem unwilling to put forth the effort to seek a degree of solitude. These same people do the majority of complaining about the river being crowded. This is compounded when late in the day floating anglers try to extend their day. When finding themselves suddenly near the boat ramp, they park their boats and join the waders near Little Hole. For float-fishermen, "crowded" is more defined as congested. When boaters all launch at the same time, clumps of boats tend to form, giving the illusion of crowding, when in reality, pressure above and below them is really very light. Again, late in the day boats tend to stack up in the lower reaches of the river for the same reason.

Certainly there are times when the river meets another definition of crowded: filled to excess. When these conditions exist they do influence, even diminish, the quality of all of our experience. The U.S. Forest Service has studied this issue, and as a result of a 1991 study *The Recreation Use Capacity of the Green River Corridor below Flaming Gorge Dam*, placed use limits on this resource for when this river approaches that definition. Since those limits are seldom reached, chances are that no one will be turned away. The Green River is a large river and handles heavy use better than other rivers. Here are a few suggestions for reducing your exposure to high river traffic.

Timing

Avoid holidays and weekends whenever possible. We consider Fridays and Saturdays as weekends on the Green River. If this is not possible, be realistic in your expectations. Try to avoid the upper canyon during peak times. This is the non-competitive approach as compared to the guy who shows up on 4th of July weekend insisting on fishing the "A" Section, then wonders why there are so many people around. The acknowledged ratio of use between the "A" Section and "B" and "C" Sections is nine to one. This makes a great case for fishing below Little Hole.

Nix the Holidays

This river's busy season is between Memorial Day and Labor Day, when school is out. During this period the river is used by white-water rafters as well as fishermen. July has two major holidays, the 4th of July and Pioneer Days (a state holiday) on July 24. Whenever possible, it is best to avoid the peak days of the holidays mentioned.

Keep On Walking

Be willing to walk. Many anglers only know a few holes close to the boat ramps. A little work can put you in contact with friendlier fish that do not see as many anglers. Close to the boat ramp you will encounter more people and more educated fish. Float fishermen should explore other launch time alternatives, avoiding the 9:00 to 11:00 a.m. peak period.

Respect

Finally, reasonable tolerance and regard for others makes any fishing excursion more pleasurable. When in doubt about whether you are crowding a fellow angler seek their permission before fishing in close proximity to them. Homesteading an area is not an uncommon practice among many anglers. While anglers should enjoy an area or a particular group of fish, they should also be considerate of others by moving on after a reasonable period of time. With the number of fish-per-mile, more are just around the river's bend. Besides, one only needs a small stretch of this river to provide great angling opportunities. Give your fellow anglers a break by practicing the "Golden Rule."

Upper River
Summer Fly Patterns

Pale Morning Duns: 14 to 18; Pheasant Tail; Floating PMD Nymph; Parachute PMD; Sparkle-Dun PMD; Yellow Humpy

Cranefly: 8 to 6; Larva; Double Ugly

Stoneflies: Brown Stone (Anderson),10; Stimulators, 8 to 10, yellow or olive

Cicadas: 8 to 10; Cricada Trude; May/June hatch; afterwards as attractors

Mormon Cricket: 4 to 6; Crystal Mormon Cricket

Fall Fly Patterns

Tricos: 20 to 22; black/white Polywing Spinner

Fall *Baetis*: 20 to 22; Pheasant Tail Nymphs; WD40, gray or olive; RSII, gray or olive; Parachute Adams

Midges: 18 to 24; Kaufmann's Chironomid; WD 40, red or black; midge larvae, red or green; Biot Midges, olive or red; Brassie, copper, red or green; Parachute Griffith's Gnat; midge adults, tan, gray, black or olive

Fly Patterns for Both Seasons

Scuds: 12 to 18; olive, amber, tan

Caddis: 8 to 18; Hare's Ear; Chamois Caddis; Soft Hackles, orange, green or peacock; Cased Caddis; Elk Hair Caddis (various body colors); Goddard Caddis

Ants: 12 to 18; Black Fur Ant; Sailor Ant; CDC Ant; Flying Ant

Cricket: 8 to 14; Parachute Cricket; Dave's Cricket; Letort Cricket

Beetles: 10 to 16; Foam Beetle; Chernobyl Ant

Grasshoppers: 6 to 12; Parachute; Dave's Hopper; Joe's Hopper

Attractors: Royal Wulffs, 8 to 18; Humpys, 8 to 18, yellow, black or red; Royal Humpy, 8 to 14; Double Humpy, 6 to 12, yellow, fluorescent orange or red; Stimulators, 6 to 12, yellow, orange or royal; Trudes, 8 to 14, Royal, Crystal, Rio Grande King; Peacock/Crystal Wiggler

Streamers: 4 to 8; Woolly Buggers, black, black/olive; ginger, brown or olive; Crystal Buggers; Zonkers, black/gold, natural/gold; Matukas; Muddler Minnows; Dark Spruce Fly; Platte River Specials

The Lower River
Spring

The lower river, as defined before, starts four miles below Little Hole at Red Creek rapids. It includes the second half of the "B" Section and all of the "C" Section with a total length of 18 miles to the Colorado State line. The dividing line between the upper and lower river is its surrounding habitat. The upper river has a rocky-gravely bottom, while the area below Red Creek consists of a siltier-sandy gravel bottom.

The lower river is slower, flatter, and warmer in nature. Its bottom is light in color and does little to conceal the movements of anglers or boats. In the upper river trout use all the habitat, in the lower river they use only areas that have abundant structure. Here, the trout and its preferred habitat are much harder to locate even to the trained eye. The trout even take on a lighter color to closely blend into their environment. They utilize the river's edges because it contains the most structure and provides opportunities for feed. The mid-river structures that dominate the upper river are sometimes far apart or completely non-existent in the lower river.

Red Creek's Contribution

What makes for such a vast difference between the upper and lower river? Red Creek's silty contribution to the lower river's habitat. Normally, only a trickle of water, and sometimes even dry, it is the major drainage for 100 square miles of unstable terrain north of the Green River. Whether it's melting snow, rain storms, or flash flooding, Red Creek contributes additional water from this basin into the Green River.

Contained within these intermittent flows is the heavy, red, silty soil that can change the river from crystal clear to reddish brown. This happens within a short distance from Red Creek's confluence with the Green River after the waters mix. Slower river sections are susceptible to this heavy sediment dropping out. This creates the silted-in river stretches that exemplify the major changes in habitat. Some lower river sections with strong flows never silt-in and have rocky gravel bottoms. In the years when Red Creek runs frequently, it may require higher flows to flush river sections with the heaviest silt buildups.

Sometimes, it seems the Red Creek basin leeches its dirty water for days after a storm. When you see how some of these heavy silt flows affect the Green River, you will be amazed that trout and insects can survive them. During these periods, the lower river should be considered unfishable. Once Red Creek's flows stop the river can restore itself very quickly. When it starts to clear, try a Woolly Bugger in the slightly stained water.

Author and guest with beautiful hopper-caught lower river brown trout.

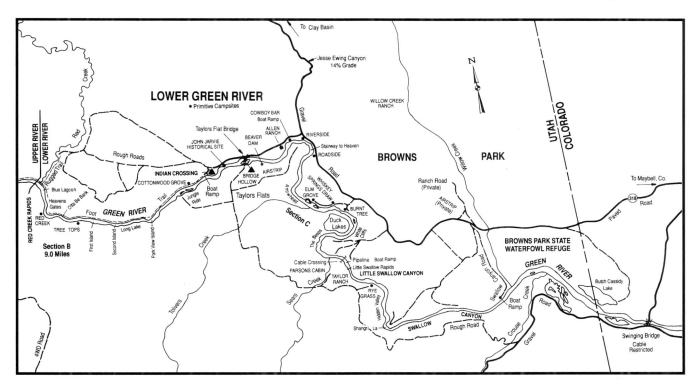

Fewer Trout

Estimates of the trout population in the lower river averages somewhere between 1500 to 3000 fish per mile. Some river sections exceed these averages, while others will fall below them. Competition for the available habitat, inconsistent hatches, siltation, varying air and water temperature ranges all result in a smaller trout population. However, far more trout exist here than is obvious (especially to the careless angler). When a major hatch occurs, trout seemingly appear from nowhere to take advantage of the available feed. There is some migration among these fish, this often results in population shifts from one area to another. Climbing water temperatures in summer is the largest stimulus for this migration.

What is so attractive about an area with so few fish? Well, there are far fewer anglers to compete with, that is always a plus! There are some beautiful stretches of river to fish. The trout are quality fish, consisting of wary wild browns, some rainbows and a few cutthroats. In size they will either be small browns or larger adult browns and rainbows 18 to 21 inches, though larger fish eight to 20 pounds are occassionally caught. Sounds like a great place to me!

Wary Trout and Cautious Approaches

The most common mistake made by wading anglers in this river section is to let their feet do more scouting than their eyes. With trout predominantly hugging the river's edge, they become extremely wary of approaching and sloppy wading anglers. These trout are best approached by not disturbing the water (with your feet) and fishing well ahead. Only after the river's prime edges have been probed should an angler make his approach by wading.

Float-fishing gives anglers the advantage of not being easily detected while approaching these trout.

Nymph fishing is the least important technique for fishing the lower river. Without being able to get close to the fish, nymph fishing may be next to impossible. Only a handful of pools in the lower river have broken water or structure that will conceal a working angler. Even there, the trout seldom stand for a sloppy approach, cast, or encroachment from an angler. Shadows and movements reflecting on a light colored river bottom assists trout in detecting the angler long before they are casted to. I have often seen these trout scooting from their lies after a careless approach. I call these fish "shooters" because they appear to shoot upstream as if from a cannon. When I see this happen, I know opportunities have been lost. It often requires considerable time before these trout can be approached again. Dry-fly fishing, with casts placed well ahead of the angler, provides the best approach to these

Lower river moose.

Red Creek with its load of Green River bound silt after a summer rainstorm.

Water and silt mix shortly after Red Creeks' confluence with the Green River.

A red silty lower river and it flows under the Taylor Flats Bridge.

The rugged basin most responsible for Red Creek's contribution.

trout. If you want to nymph fish along the river's shallow edges, try small nymphs, scuds, or emergers as a dropper below a large dry fly. Streamer fishing is very effective and covers large areas of the river while being executed from a distance. It also has the ability to "pull" fish to the fly, making areas with fewer fish less like fishing for a needle in a haystack.

Brownieville

The trout population here consists primarily of wild brown trout. It takes a tough trout strain such as the brown to thrive under the diverse conditions of this river section. Early season browns on the entire Green River are often underweight (especially females) from the physical stress of spawning in November through January. The low availability of food during the winter compounds their condition often requiring several months to regain weight. These fish are hungry and very aggressive in their effort to regain body conditioning, especially to streamers.

While the majority of the trout population here consists of beautiful browns, it is surprising how many rainbows and cutthroats can be caught when the browns are less active. Since fewer rainbows inhabit this section, their spawning activities seldom influence angling opportunities.

March

Fishing in the lower river can be good in March, but will not produce the consistent fishing found in the upper river at this time. The early season hatches are smaller and always seem to lag behind the rest of the river. Watch for trout rising on the large flats during the early season midge hatches. Later on, *Baetis* hatches will provide additional fishing opportunities. Streamers are highly effective, possibly providing the best all around approach to fishing during this early season.

April

April brings water temperature changes to the river similar to those experienced up-river. However, spring run-off in Red Creek may periodically stain the water. This staining can be light or non-existent in the mornings, but increases as the warming day melts more snow in the higher elevations.

Aquatic insect diversity increases below Red Creek, but the hatches are shorter in duration. *Baetis* and midge hatches occur with some regularity, though they will be somewhat area isolated. Early season terrestrials such as ants, small beetles and caterpillars will start appearing in some numbers, increasing their importance as trout food. Anglers should watch the river's flats for feeding trout in search of insects or continue to fish streamers.

May

In May, the angling opportunities improve with a large increase in terrestrial activity and warmer water temperatures. Aquatic hatches will continue, but the trout here are more dependent on terrestrials than on any other part of the river. Ants, beetles, small hoppers and caterpillars are

View of the Green River and Brown's Park from the Jesse Ewing canyon road.

the most common, usually finding their way into the river after changes in flows.

Fluctuating flows have less impact on the lower river than upstream river stretches because the water surge is dissipated over the miles. Besides, these browns are consummate bank huggers and practice opportunistic behavior. Slightly higher flows only increase the amount of bank area available to them.

Water temperatures will be several degrees higher than at the dam, with the water warming as it travels downstream. Do not forget that the greatest advantage to this river section is its seclusion. If you are looking for solitude and challenging wild brown trout, this may be the right choice. As with the upper river, this section will be effected by the recovery program for rare native fish by higher spring flows. See the "Green River Flows" chapter (page 52) for more detail.

Red Creek Revisited

One final note about Red Creek. Its contribution to the Green River has existed for many decades. In the pre-dam years, high spring flows removed most of its deposits. Of all the concerns for the lower river's future, the effects of Red Creek require the most investigation for possible improvements. Whether it is settling basins constructed in Clay Basin, or repairs to the riparian vegetation in areas overgrazed by livestock, something should be done to reduce Red Creek's overall impact. Unfortunately, it would be nearly impossible to completely stop its adverse effects, but reducing it would help considerably in maintaining better trout habitat. To their credit, the Bureau of Land Management has addressed some of these issues with a "Red Creek Management Plan." Some of this plan's

objectives are being worked on, however, other aspects have yet to be realized.

Some interests have proposed a monster flow released from Flaming Gorge Dam to flush the silt down-river. However, the magnitude of such a flow would certainly create scouring and may adversely effect the upper river. Since the closing of Flaming Gorge Dam, the fine sediments and nutrients that nourished the river are now accumulating in the reservoir. So the balancing act between removing the lower river's silt while preserving the upper river's environment will be an interesting feat. However it occurs, the repairing of the lower river will require the cooperation of many interested groups and government agencies. Whatever can be done will pay off big time in improved trout habitat in the lower river.

Lower River

Spring Fly Patterns

Midges: 18 to 24; Parachute Griffith's Gnat; midge adults, tan, gray, olive or black

Baetis: 16 to 20; Parachute Adams; Parachute Blue-wing Olive; Compara-dun, gray or olive

Streamers: 4 to 8; Woolly Buggers in all the normal colors. Also try ginger and brown

Spring Terrestrials: (late April-May); ants, 12 to 18; beetles, 14 to 16; hoppers, 12 to 14

Others: Royal Wulffs, 14 to 18; Rio Grande King Trudes, 14; Crystal Trudes, 14; Elk Hair Caddis, 14 to 16

Lower River
Summer/Fall

Author's note: While this chapter deals with the lower river in summer, please read the "Lower River/Spring" chapter (page 44). It has valuable information for anyone planning to fish this portion of the river.

Water Temperature and Migration

In the heat of summer the lower river's air and water temperatures can climb steadily through the day. Here, the slower, shallower, river with its lighter colored bottom and clear water, produces greater thermal warming than the upper river stretches. Water temperatures also warm as the river travels farther from the dam as the air temperatures extract the river's coolness. The disparity between the temperature of water released from the dam and what the temperature is down-river is greatest in the summer. Water temperatures down-river can reach into the high 60s during summer months. Low volume river flows will increase this effect making it tough to fish in the heat of the day.

Trout respond to these long days of excessive heat by sulking during the warmest periods of the day. Brown trout detest bright sunlight and heat, often seeking relief by migrating out of marginal areas into the riffles, shady areas, and deeper holes. These are the best places to fish because the deeper holes provide cooler water temperatures and moving water adds oxygen. So, when you locate a few trout, remember there are probably others congregated there.

To counter the heat's effect, try fishing in the cooler times of the day, either early, late, when it is cloudy, just after a rain, or watch for a change in water flows. Even the slightest change in flow often brings a response or different attitude from the trout. This increase in water volume provides cooler water temperatures and increases the number of insects available to trout. Ants are a great example of an insect that gets flushed from the river's grassy banks.

Low Tolerance

While the lower river is capable of some great fishing, it does not deal well with lots of angling pressure. Luckily, it does not receive this pressure and is therefore a great place to avoid the summer rafters on the "A" Section.

Contrary to the trout up-river, once spooked lower river trout require time to recover. Remember, the majority of these fish are wary wild brown trout. Too many boats or anglers in this river section reduces the success rate for all. Two to four boats floating in close proximity to each other is too much pressure. It is best when you can plan to be one of the few boats or wading anglers on this section. Then keep as much space possible between you and others.

We Hear You

On numerous occasions, Green River brown trout have exhibited a great sensitivity to sound. This is especially true of the browns in the lower river section. When a large

Float-fishing Little Swallow Canyon. Emmett Heath photo.

fly is presented, it often makes a splat on the water. This either attracts the trout or spooks them. Indeed, I have seen brown trout move ten feet to inspect the fly. Anglers often pull the fly away from a trout just arriving to investigate the source of that "splat." Then, as the angler picks up the line and fly, the trout is spooked. So be patient in allowing time for the trout to respond to each presentation.

When the fly lands near them these trout may be cautious, watching the fly from their in-stream station. Often they will let the fly drift past their position before slowly coming up to follow or inspect it. Is it because they are trying to assure themselves it is a real insect, or do they know anglers are often impatient? In both cases, the lesson is to leave the fly on the water for a reasonable period of time. Make the cast, then wait to see what comes.

The Green just below Red Creek Rapids.

June

Trout in this river section have to work hard to gather enough food to survive, this makes them very vulnerable. Like the upper river in summer, my most common approach is with terrestrials—ants, beetles, crickets, caterpillars, and hoppers. They are effective throughout this season.

By June, hoppers are much larger physically and are at their peak in abundance and variety. Summer attractor dry flies consist of large temptations such as Royal Wulffs, standard Stimulators, Royal Stimulators, Double Uglys, and Royal or Yellow Humpys. Remember that large, black, and shiny is very effective. Patterns with these qualities include Chernobyl Ants, Crystal Cripplers and Crystal Trudes.

Anglers should also watch for cicadas and Mormon crickets on the lower river. Though cicadas are usually not significant as a hatch below Red Creek, their patterns still fit the large, shiny, black criteria and are useful as attractor patterns.

The appearance of Mormon crickets anywhere along the lower river corridor is a welcomed sight. For more information on this periodical visitor to the Green River see the "Insects of the Green River" chapter (page 60). I highly recommend, that anglers try different tandem fly combinations between the larger attractor or terrestrial patterns and the smaller ones. Late June will also find Pale Morning Duns and caddis hatching.

July and August

While the Green River has many beautiful days during this season it also has its share of windy days. In the openness of Browns Park, hot afternoon winds have little to slow them down. In July and August, hefty breezes will place grasshoppers, damsels, and other food sources in the water. Heavier weight rods are often beneficial for throwing the large flies fished on a gusty summer day. The terrestrials and attractors patterns previously discussed will continue their effectiveness. My overall favorite is the size 10 Royal Wulff or Humpy. Keep in mind this is brown trout territory and they love these kinds of flies.

Caddis patterns always work well in the lower river. Elk Hair Caddis patterns size 10 to 16 are productive, body colors can range from peacock, tan, orange and olive. While these patterns work well for the hours before dusk and dawn when caddis are active, they are also great used as attractors anytime.

Insect-sipping trout can often be sighted on the large flats, such as Burnt Tree. These fish work in pods and actively move up and down the middle of the flats. Though there is not much midge activity at this time of year, a well-placed Griffith's Gnat always produces strikes from these trout.

Damselflies are prolific in the Browns Park section because of several large impoundments used for waterfowl management adjacent to the river. Summer trout do exhibit some interest in these active insects.

A beautiful Swallow Canyon brown trout.

September and October

As things cool down in September and October, fishing remains fairly consistent. The importance of the terrestrial to both the trout and the angler does not diminish until the snow starts flying. A dropper ant or beetle fished with a larger dry is still a successful combination.

In slower fishing situations, try experimenting by changing wing silhouettes. When fishing upwing patterns such as a large Wulff or Humpy brings little success, try a down wing such as a Trude. This change has saved me on many slow days. Streamers will also bring some nice trout to the net. Woolly Buggers in sizes 8 to 4 are very effective, you will have to experiment for the color of the day.

The fall *Baetis* return on the cooler days, but do not depend on hatches on this river section. When hatches occur, great! But you will move more fish consistently on attractors and terrestrials. River *Callibaetis,* can occasionally be found hatching around Cable Crossing. They usually occur mid-morning. Caddis will also remain important during these months with hatches of several species occurring somewhat regularly.

October is an underrated time to fish the Green River. This river section receives even lighter use, though it fishes well then. Many people have gone home, leaving a degree of solitude for those anglers remaining. For many of us, this may the best month of all to fish, with trout actively feeding and cooler water and air temperatures.

Pesky Critters

The large impoundments used for waterfowl habitat in Browns Park attract mosquitoes and deer flies. The mosquitoes are not normally a big problem unless you camp at night in Browns Park. Common repellent works very well on them. However, the deer flies in the hot summer and fall months can be pesky, even ferocious. They pester

floaters but not as much as the bank wade fishermen who disturb the bankside vegetation. They love exposed skin and insect repellents are often ineffective. The most effective deterrent to their bite is to cover up bare skin and limit disturbing the riverside vegetation.

Browns Park State Waterfowl Refuge

Browns Park also contains a Utah Division of Wildlife Resources Waterfowl Management Area in Utah and a wildlife refuge in Colorado, both provide for an abundance of waterfowl in the area. Geese and ducks are hunted in October and November along the river corridor. Many hunters combine trout fishing with their bird hunting for a "cast and blast" routine.

Lower River

Summer Fly Patterns

Pale Morning Duns: 14 to 18; Pheasant Tail; Floating PMD Nymph; Parachute PMD; Sparkle Dun PMD; Yellow Humpy

Fall Fly Patterns

Midges: 18 to 24; Parachute Griffith's Gnat; midge adults, tan, gray, olive or black

Tricos: 20 to 22; black/white Polywing Spinner

Fall *Baetis:* 20 to 22; Pheasant Tail Nymph; WD40; RSII, grey or olive; Sparkle Duns, gray or olive; Parachute Adams

Fly Patterns for Both Seasons

Caddis: 8 to 18; Elk Hair Caddis (various body colors)

Ants: 12 to 18; Black Fur Ant; Sailor Ant; CDC Ant; Flying Ant

Cricket: 10 to 14; Parachute Cricket; Dave's Cricket; Letort Cricket

Beetles: 10 to 16; Foam Beetle; Chernobyl Ant

Grasshoppers: 6 to 12; Parachute; Dave's Hopper; Joe's Hopper

Attractors: Royal Wulffs, 8 to 18; Humpys, 8 to 18, yellow, black or red; Royal Humpy, 8 to 14; Double Humpy, 6 to 12, yellow, fluorescent orange or red; Stimulators, 6 to 12, yellow, orange or royal; Trudes, 8 to 14, Royal, Crystal, Rio Grande King; Peacock/Crystal Wiggler

Streamers: 4 to 8; Woolly Buggers, black, black/olive, ginger, brown or olive; Crystal Buggers; Zonkers, black/gold, natural/gold; Matukas; Muddler Minnows; Dark Spruce Fly; Platte River Specials

The Green River In Winter

Winter along the Green River is a time of solitude. Bald eagles grace the barren riverside trees, and large herds of wintering deer and elk are seen on the way to and from the river. There are many days when it is possible not to encounter another angler! Even better are the beautiful trout you can catch amidst these spectacular settings. The factors that most influence winter fishing are water temperature, periods of sunlight, river flow and opportunities to feed.

The Winter Approach

The river and its edges never freeze and the access roads are plowed after each snow. The canyon walls and nearby hillsides are often snow-covered, but the river trails rarely have any snow on them. Certain stretches of the river have limited periods of sunlight and it is chilly in the shadowed areas. In the morning it is best to allow several hours for the sun to warm the river's air. I usually approach the river after 9:00 or 10:00 a.m. and quit by 5:00 p.m. in the short days of winter (December through February). In March, the days become a little longer providing a few more fishing hours.

November

In November, the river's water temperature will still be high enough (46 to 48 degrees) for the fish to actively feed. These temperatures are possible because the reservoir lags behind the weather in cooling its water. Some dry flies can be used, but scuds, midges, nymphs, and streamers are the big producers. Specific fly patterns and size recommendations are the same as those for March.

Air temperatures will be dropping to average 45 degrees. Brown trout are generally actively spawning by mid-month and will continue through December and even into January. They are well distributed along the river, but are most numerous from Little Hole to Browns Park. Streamers are always effective for spawning browns.

Changes in Water Temperature

When water temperatures drop (44 to 42 degrees) further in December, it starts the reversal of what occurs in

Angling opportunities exist in the colder months. Jim French photo.

the spring. Trout become more dormant with many podding in certain areas of the river. This will mean fishing deep and directly to the fish. For the months with low water temperatures, I must emphasize, "fish the trout, not the water." Scuds and midge larvae again become the trout's major table fare. Watch for those extraordinary midge hatches that occur during the winter, they are especially strong during long stretches of warmer blue sky days. Occasionally even a few *Baetis* will hatch on a winter's day.

Daytime high temperatures are most often around 36 to 45 degrees with many beautiful days between the snow-bearing storm fronts. Though in tougher winters temperatures can range from the single digits to the teens for the daytime highs.

Skiers visiting the many great winter resorts in Utah/Colorado often take breaks to spend a few days winter trout fishing on the Green River. Local lodges and guide services often discount rates for their services to encourage business at this time of year. For fishing you will want to layer your clothing and dress very warmly.

January and February

January and February will bring more days of sunshine than stormy ones, in a ratio usually higher than three to one. The daytime high air temperature will average 25 to 45 degrees, however many sunny days reach into the 50s. Water temperatures can drop to 38 to 41 degrees.

The river is extremely quiet at this time of year, though fishing is still very productive with scuds and midges. Try slowly stripping, even dead-drifting, Woolly Buggers in white or pink in sizes 4 to 6, for the more aggressive fish. The brown trout from Little Hole down to Browns Park strongly approve of this approach as shown by their hard strikes.

Winter Flows

When there is excess storage in the reservoir going into the fall the Bureau of Reclamation will dump water. This results in higher than normal river flows through the winter to prepare the reservoir for inflows from spring run-off. In drought years, the winter flows will normally be low, as water is conserved for use the following year. Most winter flows are either stable or have one fluctuation a day. These flows provide good fishing even when they may be high volume releases. The worst possible thing for trout in winter are fluctuating flows that require them to use up valuable body reserves continually adjusting to changes in flows.

While there are always trout to be caught during this season, it is probably best to make local inquiries about the winter flows before coming. Winter trout fishing provides a great opportunity to experience the Green River as few people ever see it. I highly recommend it!

Green River Flows

This two part chapter will discuss the operation of Flaming Gorge Dam and what anglers need to know in dealing with different flows.

Part One

The Operation of Flaming Gorge Dam

In preparing this guide, dealing with river flows as released from Flaming Gorge Dam with its complex physical, economic, environmental, political, and social issues, presented the greatest challenge. The competition for the limited resources created by the operation of this dam seem to accelerate every year. This competition comes from various federal and state government agencies and other interests revolving around water, power, recreation, fish and wildlife. Why should anglers be concerned about the competition from these various user groups? Of concern is what will be the priority level assigned to this trout fishery and the aquatic environment that it needs to survive when weighed against other uses?

In the future, we anglers need to be more active and vigilant than ever in competing for and protecting the places that represent our values. The competition is well organized and financed. Are we? The Green River and its tailwater trout fishery will need friends if it is to be protected and remain one of the top trout rivers in the world.

The Paradox

Ed Engle in his book *Fly Fishing the Tailwaters* called tailwater fisheries a "paradox." He is right! The fact that you are fly fishing in great trout water landing a hefty rainbow is wonderful, but in many places it would not be possible except for the massive man-made concrete structure that created suitable trout habitat. The Green River tailwater trout fishery was the creation that resulted from the construction of Flaming Gorge Dam completed in 1963. There were few, if any, trout in this river stretch prior to the dam. The trout that did find their way into this region of the river probably came from area tributaries such as Sheep Creek. Clearly today's quality Green River trout fishery would not exist without the Flaming Gorge Dam.

The Ups and Downs

As anglers we tend to look at what benefits us from the creation of fisheries below dams. While paradoxes can be good, they also can be bad. The way a dam is operated can either give you great angling opportunities or it can take them away. On the positive side, tailwaters provide controlled flows, moderated impacts of spring run-off, sustained in-stream flows during droughts, improved water quality, and in the case of the Flaming Gorge Dam, regulated water temperatures to benefit trout and invertebrates.

On the negative side, released flows can be high, fluctuating, radical, and unpredictable. They can have profound effects on trout, invertebrates, water quality, water temperatures, and angling opportunities. Dams can also be operated in ways that are not consistent with maintaining a tailwater trout fishery. While this trout fishery was created with the construction of the Flaming Gorge Dam, its future existence is totally dependent on how this dam is operated.

The Physical Operational Parameters

Flaming Gorge Dam is capable of ranging its releases from a minimal flow of 800 cfs (cubic feet/second) to a maximum generation flow of 4800 cfs with ramping rates of

DIVISION BY RIVER WATER FLOWS	
FULL GEN.+BYPASS	8800 CFS
FULL GENERATION	4800 CFS
HIGH FLOW	2800 CFS
MINIMUM FLOW	800 CFS

500 cfs per minute. While the dam is capable of putting out 4800 cfs, maximum generation is usually kept around 4400 to 4500 cfs to prevent damage to the overall structure. The 800 cfs minimum in-stream flow is provided by an agreement between Utah Division of Wildlife Resources and the Bureau of Reclamation for maintaining the trout fishery.

The dam has the additional ability to release up to

Flaming Gorge Dam.

2,000 cfs through each of two bypass tubes and an additional 28,800 cfs through the spillway overflow. To date the bypass tubes have been sparingly used, only during generator maintenance or in times of severe flooding that threatened the dam. This occurred in 1983,1984, 1986 and 1997. The highest releases from the Flaming Gorge Dam were in 1983 at approximately 13,000 cfs because of a record snowpack overfilling the reservoir and involved using both the bypass tubes and spillway overflow.

Economics

In the years following construction of the dam, the patterns of the releases into the Green River were developed with power generation marketing as a priority. This resulted in large fluctuating flows in summer and winter when massive volumes of water suddenly released created peak powering that results in top dollar electricity. Any angler who fishes tailwater rivers has experienced these peak power surges and knows how they effect angling opportunities.

The management of this hydroelectric dam falls on two federal agencies, the Bureau of Reclamation (Reclamation) who handles reservoir storage and monthly releases from the dam and the Western Area Power Administration (Western) who markets the electricity produced and determines daily and hourly releases. Trout were not always a priority when it came to the operation

of this dam. However, in recent years there has been movement by both Reclamation and Western to consider the issues of tailwater trout fisheries. This is, in part, due to the experiences gained at Glen Canyon Dam on the Colorado River. This dam's operations for power generation and the resulting environmental effects created court injunctions, lawsuits, costly studies, and low public opinion. This took a great toll on both agencies; today their approach is through negotiated solutions to problems created by the operation of their dams.

The difficult management of the issues and interests surrounding the operation of Flaming Gorge Dam is handled by Reclamation. This has been accomplished by the creation of work groups with one representative from each interest group and public involvement. The Green River Outfitter and Guides Association (GROGA) has taken an active role as representatives of trout issues within the Flaming Gorge Work Group and other public forums.

Environmental Politics and the Threatened and Endangered Fishes

The U.S. Fish and Wildlife Service (Service) is charged with recovering endangered native Colorado River fish under the Endangered Species Act of 1973 (ESA). The ESA has potential conflicts with existing laws such as the Colorado River Storage Projects Act of 1956 which authorized construction of the Flaming Gorge Dam.

In 1992 Service biologists issued a biological opinion

that started a five-year study to gather data for a recovery program for the rare native Colorado River fish, which include the Colorado River squawfish, boneytail and humpback chubs, and razorback suckers. Many factors have contributed to the decline of these rare native fishes. However, biologists are pointing to the construction and operation of the Flaming Gorge Dam as one of many culprits. They emphasize that with spring run-offs under control of the dam, the natural annual hydrography (ups and downs) of the river were interrupted.

The Pre-dam River

Traditionally, high spring flows occurred on the Green and Yampa rivers upstream from Jensen, Utah from early May through June depending on winter snowpack in the mountains. These flows flooded many riverside backwater areas that provided habitat for the recruitment of native fishes. They also provided the flushing, cleansing flows that kept the river healthy and created the riparian habitat along the pre-dam river. Environmental changes have occurred in the river's bed since the completion of Flaming Gorge Dam with its controlled flows. Alluvial processes have covered many of the old river gravel bars creating a narrower river that has been overtaken by streamside vegetation. These stands of tamarisk are in stark contrast to the traditional cottonwood groves of the old river. From late June (except for flash floods from rainstorms, etc.) when the river receded it ran a constant flow averaging 400 cfs for the balance of the year. Accompanying this lower flow was the resulting warmer water temperatures.

The Recovery Program

Though the "Final Biological Opinion for the Re-Operation of Flaming Gorge Dam" has not been completed at the time of this printing, some aspects of the Service's recovery program are unfolding. The thrust of their approach is to mimic the traditional natural river hydrography as closely as possible, including high spring and lower summer releases from Flaming Gorge Dam.

The trigger to start spring flows is the start of spring run-off from the Yampa River, an undammed tributary of the Green River. Combined flows from Yampa and Green rivers provide flows for the critical habitat areas of native fish. These flows are monitored at Jensen, Utah's gauging station.

Flow Scenarios

Different flow volumes and durations have been examined. Most proposals involve running Flaming Gorge Dam at maximum generation (4700 cfs) for a period of time that is dependent on water availability. The use of the by-pass tubes to create larger flows of up to 8800 cfs is still controversial at this time. However, it is GROGA'S hope that these flows will only occur as an act of nature and not of man.

At issue is whether this river biologically needs a periodical flushing, such as the one that occurred in 1996 at Glen Canyon Dam. There is some scientific evidence pointing in this direction. However, those that were so quick to announce the "experiment" at Glen Canyon as a

The Green River at its minimal flow of 800 cfs.

"huge success" need to realize that its long term effects will need years of further evaluation to determine its real value as an environmental tool. With these flushing flows, there is the real possibility of environmental damage from the scouring of the vegetation that aquatic invertebrates depend on. A reduction in the river's insect biomass would certainly effect trout populations and their survival. Should this flow be allowed on a regular basis, accumulative damage to the aquatic environment could cause the decline of this trout fishery.

In low water (drought) years, flows of 4700 cfs are one to two weeks in duration while in ample water (wet) years they could last up to six weeks. Forecasts of proposed flows are possible in April after winter snowpack and most probably water supply figures are evaluated by Reclamation. Typically flows will be ramped up or down in increments leveling off at each target flow. Both of these changes in flow takes around one week each. After reaching the peak (ramping up), flows are supposed to be stable. Our experience shows that this is not always so, with the possibility of some daily fluctuations.

Following the high spring flows, summer flows should average 800 to 1600 cfs at Flaming Gorge dam through October. These flows again are mimicking the river's natural hydrography and are great for trout fishing. After October, winter flows will vary depending on the need to regulate storage in the reservoir for the following spring. Our guess is that winter flow requests should be for the stable, non-fluctuating flows that are good for trout as well as native fish.

GROGA has identified the following issues dealing with trout and the operation of Flaming Gorge Dam. We are concerned that: high flows should be stable, not fluctuating, ramping rates should be executed slowly up and down. Flows should not exceed the capacity of the power plant of 4700 cfs (no monster flows) except in an emergency. Bypass flows should only occur as an act of nature, and their frequency should be kept at an absolute minimum. High flows on wintering trout should be

The same river pool at 4500 cfs, an 8800 cfs flow would nearly bury all of the large rocks pictured.

minimized, but when necessary they should be stable. Existing minimal flow agreements pertaining to the trout fishery should not be violated.

Social Issues

While the evolution of flows on the Green River below Flaming Gorge Dam is still unfolding, the final disposition of this blue-ribbon trout river is in all of our hands. Together we will have to decide whether this trout fishery is of value and worth protecting, or if we should give it away to other uses? A balancing of uses is most desirable, but without vigilance our values will not be heard above the rhetoric of those who would dismiss this "irreplaceable national treasure" for reasons of their own.

Part Two

Fishing the High Flows

Now that we have finished our crash course on the "politics" of flows, what does this mean for the average Green River angler? It means that anglers will need to be well informed as to the possible flows they might encounter and how to approach them.

Though it may be prudent to check on flows before a visit, in late winter and spring it is imperative! Local sources such as lodges, guide services and tackle shops will provide the most accurate up-to-date information. Many Internet sites for fly fishermen offer current river reports, or you might call the Bureau of Reclamations' River Flow Information at 1-800-277-7571. This number will provide you with flow information for many rivers in several western states, however, it will not tell you about the fishing.

Fishing Flows

As stated in the introduction to the "Green River Fly Fishing Calendar" the flows usually average between

800-2800 cfs. For approaches to the river during these flows, consult that portion of this guide. If allowed to choose I would ask for flows of 1800 to 2400 cfs for what I consider optimal fishing. For the purpose of discussion we will consider flows 2800-4700 cfs as "high generation" flows and those above this (4700-8800 cfs or more) as "monster" flows. High generation flows are the river levels which change where the fish will be found in the river; how best to access them might differ from normal approaches. These are still great flows for fishing when the trout have had time to acclimate and water quality is decent. Monster flows, depending on their severity, may or may not be a good time to fish. As we experience more of these extreme flows, their effects on angling opportunities will become more clear.

Compared with a minimum in-stream flow of 800 cfs what does 4700 cfs look like? In the "A" Section, 4700 cfs adds nearly five vertical feet of water to the existing river elevation. With the "B" and "C" sections the impact is lessened because of the additional river bed width, and adds around four vertical feet. An 8800 cfs flow adds an additional four-and-one-half vertical feet of river elevation to the high generation flow (eight to nine feet above minimal flow).

Flow Benchmarks

When you approach the river at the Spillway or at Little Hole, you can roughly figure out the water flow level by looking at the concrete boat ramps. The bottom of these ramps were set near the minimum flow levels of 800 cfs. As the water rises above this point it creeps up the concrete slab. A non-scientific approach to figuring the cfs of a flow is to start with the 800 cfs at the bottom of the ramp, then add 1000 cfs for every 16 vertical inches of water depth above that level. This approach should get you close enough for practical purposes. Minimum low flows will expose much of the river's cover and it takes on

To determine river flows, monitor the boat ramps. The lowest point on the concrete ramp was set at minimal flow of 800 cfs elevation.

Dried exposed moss or water marks on the rocks often show recent flow histories. A wet or disappearing rock will reveal hourly changes in flows. Wading anglers should locate a reference rock to visually monitor while wading, watching for changes in flows that could jeopardize their safety.

a spring creek type of appearance. Exposed moss beds with their tops right at water level, or living algae on the rocks showing four to six inches, are indicative of flows lower than recent flow history.

Smaller Fluctuations

Not all changes in flow reach the 4700 cfs level. Smaller daily or hourly fluctuations of 18 inches or less give trout a shorter timeframe to adjust, and in the most severe cases, they could be affected for up to two hours. If this flow change has not been a part of their daily routine, it may well upset the trout's world. They do not deal well with sudden, rapid changes in flows. Each change can result in their needing to leave preferred habitat because of change in current velocities and the energy requirement needed to match this change. Their response to these movements in flow requires time for them to adjust to this newly created environment. Additionally, increased energy expenditures often result in stress for trout, this can be lethal for wintering trout whose energy reserves are at their lowest.

If you notice a decrease in the fishing when these changes occur, take a break until the trout re-orientate themselves. Often, as the water ascends, insects become dislodged in the stronger current's drift. This stimulus often results in the trout returning to feeding.

Descending flows reduce the number of insects and has the opposite effect by shutting down feeding activity. Do not confuse these smaller fluctuating flows with descending flows from a period of high stable flows. Each lowering of the river will require time for the trout to once again re-distribute themselves throughout the river as their environment is reduced.

Water Quality

Increasing water flows initially produce some floating debris such as pine needles, sticks, and moss as the river rises. This is especially true when going to an extremely high flow after extended periods of low flows. In severe cases when the debris is substantial it can accumulate, clogging up many of the larger backwater areas.

In early spring, water quality can be additionally compromised by the dying, feathering moss beds breaking apart with higher flows. While these are the worst possible effects of higher flows, conditions do improve after several days of flushing.

Angling opportunities can be effected during this period by compounding poor water quality with the displacement of the trout population due to higher flows. This brief period is the worst possible time for anglers on the river. They will have to wait for the water quality to improve and the trout to adjust to their new environment, usually signaled by their return to feeding.

Should you find yourself fishing the river when a major change in flow occurs, try to visually locate trout to fish for. Some areas of the river are less effected by changes in flows, so trout adjust quicker in those places. Look along the river's slower edges and in the smaller open backwater areas that provide trout with a refuge from the stronger currents and debris.

The dams two "bypass tubes" in use. Each is capable of releasing an additional 2000 cfs. This picture does not show the additional water that can be released by spilling through the dam's overflow gates.

High Stable Flows

Should high flows up to 4700 cfs discourage you? Not at all! In fact, you may be passing up some top fishing. Water quality and flow stability are the most critical factors to consider in evaluating fishing potential. After the initial rising of the river, water quality improves after a short period of flushing. Steady high flows, or those with moderate fluctuations, provide trout an opportunity to adjust to their environment. It will mean that river levels might be less than your ideal, but do not make the mistake of dismissing the river. Opportunities for exceptional trout fishing still exist. Sure, there is additional water volume added to an already deep and powerful river. The currents will be stronger, the runs much deeper, however, because of this river's large pool/small pool nature, the trout have somewhere to escape from the stronger river areas.

Debris gathering in the river's back-eddies is one of the most noticeable changes in the river after a drastic change in flows.

With high flows these pools become deeper and larger and tend to concentrate trout. While higher flows will take away some fishing areas familiar to anglers, it often creates new trout habitat and opportunities elsewhere. Look for the new places along the river that hold trout.

These flows most effect the wading angler in his ability to physically wade around in the river, which I must point out is somewhat restricted because of the river's overall depth even at its lowest levels. This wading restriction is not a handicap to anglers. After all, the trout become more concentrated from being pushed into the river's slower edges and pools where they often become readily accessible from the shoreline. Boats add immeasurably to the versatility in accessing more fish in high water. One difficulty with floating in high flows is that the time required to drift a river section is reduced sharply. Floaters will have to pace themselves, possibly spending some time wading parts of the river. The nymph float-fishing techniques previously discussed will all be useful during this time. Try the "outrigger" or "dredge" techniques for shallow to medium deep water (ten feet deep), and the "down and across" technique for the deeper runs.

Fishing the Higher Flows

The most consistent productive fishing during high flow periods is nymphing. Knowing where the trout lie and the effective patterns to use during these flows are certainly an advantage. Start by looking for trout in areas of the river that are low to medium velocity. Other good prospects for trout are areas with large back eddies, under foamy slicks, shallow riffles and slower river edges with

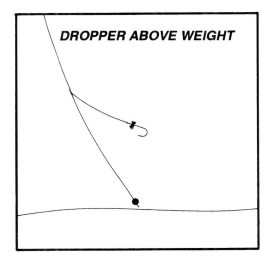

DROPPER ABOVE WEIGHT

good structure. For high flow, deep nymphing, use longer leaders of 12 feet or more. Large, colorful, weighted flies such as beadhead scuds and cranefly larvae with various trailers are also in order.

When trout can be observed suspended, try suspending nymphs at their level with a strike indicator or large dry fly. One rigging for high water, float nymph fishing, is to place a reasonably large split shot at the bottom of the tippet and have one or two dropper flies above it. When anglers use an extremely large split shot or excessive lead we call this "cannonballing." Though this is not a great rigging for a fly rod it can be effective in the deeper river runs or used with a spinning rod.

High Flows and Dry Flies

Dry-fly fishing during higher river flows can range from excellent to poor. Study the river closely for opportunities to dry-fly fish. Great places to prospect for surface-feeding trout are in the slow water areas such as large or small backwater areas and shallow riffles. By observing them, you may be able to determine what they are feeding on and how to approach them.

If there is the stimulus of an adult aquatic hatch or terrestrials, such as *Baetis* or cicadas, tremendous dry-fly fishing can occur during these flows. This type of stimulus has occurred during many of the recent high flow years. Remember, that trout are going to take advantage of an opportunity to feed, no matter what the river flows are.

Anglers should also keep in mind the importance of terrestrial imitations and the success of attractor flies in difficult fishing conditions. If there is total disinterest in the trout to surface feed, nymph or streamer fishing may be your best choice.

Green River High-Flow Fly Patterns

Scuds: 8 to 12; orange, tan or pink; weighted
Midges: 16 to 20; Brassies, copper or red; midge larva, red or green; WD 40, red
Aquatic Worms: San Juan Worm, red, wine or brown; Green River Worm, red or brown
Craneflies: 4 to 8; Cranefly Larva
Others: WD 40, olive, gray, 16 to 20; Hare's Ear, 14 to 18

Note: Try Bead-head and Flashback versions of the above patterns. Bead heads give the fly the ability to sink quicker, Flashbacks will draw more attention. Should a midge, *Baetis*, or cicada hatch occur during these higher flows, see the recommended fly patterns for these insects in this book. Also look for opportunities to fish terrestrials and attractor flies.

Streamers: 2 to 6; all recommended patterns

Wading and Floating the Green River

Wading Tips

Wading can be a safe and effective approach to fishing the Green River. However, be aware that the Green's water clarity will disguise its real depths and what appears wadeable is sometimes an illusion. Waders should use caution never to step into one of its many deep holes. I often describe the Green River as, "ankle to knee deep or over your head."

Though not recommended, at low flows you may be able to wade across the river in a few places. If you do, choose carefully! Make sure any place you cross can also be crossed on your return. It is possible to get trapped on the other side during fluctuating river flows, higher water releases will create stronger currents and deeper water.

Your options on how to return to the other bank could be limited, one possibility is finding someone in a boat coming down the river that is willing to take you back across. Drownings have occurred when people pushed their luck. Several occurred after flow changes resulted in higher river levels.

Anglers will often use small conveyances to get across the river; rafts, a drift boat, canoe, or sometimes a float tube. Whatever device is used, it should be tied down or placed high and dry. Increased water flows can sweep away a boat left untethered.

Wading the crystal clear Green River. Larry Castruita photo.

Floating Tips

Often I have mentioned this river is perfect for fishing from a boat. In fact, it is a "floater's dream." Float-fishing gives you many advantages over wading. The primary advantage is in providing complete access to fish in all types of water. In particular, those hard to access

Use caution when floating any part of the river. The large center rock shown here in Little Steamboat Rapid has taken several lives.

non-wadeable waters, center of river runs and large back eddies that can only be accessed by floating. Other benefits to float-fishing any river are:
- Learn and experience entire river sections
- Provides waders with transportation from run to run
- Access for a physically challenged angler
- Casting from a stable platform
- Back-casting without obstruction
- Extending drag-free drifts
- Sharing fishing experiences with others

River Watercraft

Drift boats and rafts with rowing frames are the safest and most common watercraft in use on the Green River. Low-sided vessels such as john boats and canoes are not commonly used because of the river's rapids. An experienced canoeist can negotiate this river, however,

Disaster at Mother-In-Law Rapid. All types of vessels are capable of being sunk in the river's strongest runs, for your safety wear your life jackets.

many inexperienced ones have wrapped their canoes around rocks.

Hulled craft (including folding boats) are not suitable for this river. Personal floatation devices such as float tubes are allowed but not recommended for river use due to several drownings. The one-man kick boats are an improvement over standard float tubes. The operator sits higher on the water providing a better view of river obstacles, multi-vessel control options, and less body exposure. However, users of these types of vessels should check with the manufacturer before using them on rivers. No matter what type of vessel you use, nothing replaces common sense when it comes to river safety. Proper river etiquette is also a desirable and necessary boating skill.

Rapids on the "A" Section

Do not be misled by the fact that the U.S. Forest Service has classified the "A" Section of the Green River as a novice run. There are areas where even experienced boaters familiar with this river have gotten into trouble. Floaters should never take anything for granted. It only requires one large boulder falling into the river to change a rapid forever.

When in doubt about a rapid in the "A" Section, stay just right of the river's center until you can see your way through it. When you are still not quite sure which path to take, wait for another boat to float through the stretch showing you a possible safe passageway.

Bridge Rapid at 4500 cfs. At high flows, the river is at its biggest and strongest.

The first four miles on the Green River are relatively slow and flat, with a few large Class II-III rapids. Beware, many of the river's larger rapids are "boat eaters." Extra care should be exercised in Little Steamboat and Bridge Rapids. Little Steamboat has a large midstream boulder that has taken several lives.

From river-mile four to mile six there is a series of rapids and heavy water. Caution should be exercised in all of them, especially in higher flows when the water is strong. Two rapids that have potential for disaster are Mother-In-Law and Deadman rapids. Currently, only Mother-In-Law has a sign forewarning you. Deadman Rapid has a midstream rock appropriately named "suicide rock."

Clearance under the Taylor Flats Bridge is diminished at higher flows. The south portal (right-hand side looking downstream) has the most clearance, but even it may not be safe at higher flows.

Rapids on the "B" Section

Another large rapid that requires extreme caution is Red Creek Rapids. This Class III-IV is the only major rapid in the "B" Section of the Green River. Many canoes, rafts, and drift boats have been lost here. Four miles below Little Hole, a riverside sign forewarns boaters. Even those familiar with this rapid should remember it is a different class of rapid at each water level. At low levels it is a minefield of rocks with only two possible runs. The safest path is to the left, but do not take anything for granted. Use caution, get out of the boat and scout the run thoroughly, then portage if you have any doubt at all. Many commercial companies require guests to walk around this rapid. During periods of high water it is powerful, respect it!

Floating the "C" Section

The "C" Section has one major obstacle, Taylor Flats bridge. This concrete structure has little clearance for floaters at normal flows and should be approached cautiously. During higher flows it may be necessary to portage. The right side of the bridge provides the most clearance.

- See "Appendix B" (page 74) for Green River boating regulations.
- If you are new to floating rivers review "Appendix C," titled "Float-Fishing Etiquette" (page 75) in the back of this book. It provides some conflict-reducing "guidelines" for river users.

Insects of the Green River

*M*ost tailwater fisheries have some traits in common when it comes to their aquatic invertebrates. Species size and diversity are usually small, but those that exist flourish. River conditions as created by the dam's operation determine whether a species is abundant or even exists at all. For example, prior to the construction of Flaming Gorge Dam there were about 23 known species of mayfly in this section of the Green River, today there are only four well documented species. It would seem that these four species were able to adapt to the post-dam

Aquatic Insects	Terrestrials
Mayflies	Ants
Midges	Beetles
Scuds	Cicadas
Caddis	Mormon Crickets
Stoneflies	Grasshoppers
Aquatic Worms	Crickets

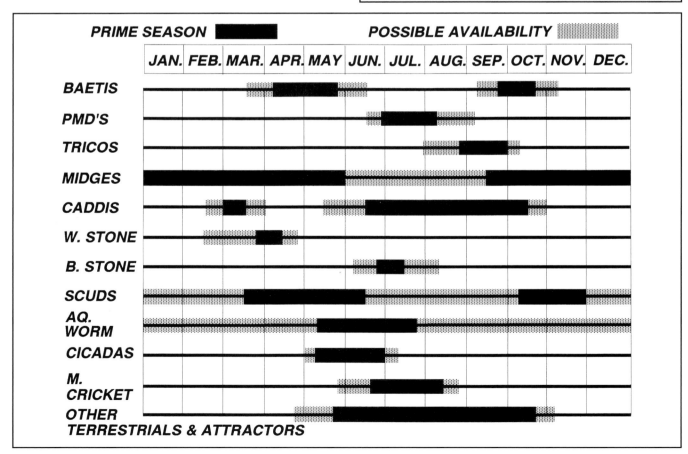

PRIME SEASON ▮▮▮   POSSIBLE AVAILABILITY ▒▒▒

	JAN.	FEB.	MAR.	APR.	MAY	JUN.	JUL.	AUG.	SEP.	OCT.	NOV.	DEC.
BAETIS												
PMD'S												
TRICOS												
MIDGES												
CADDIS												
W. STONE												
B. STONE												
SCUDS												
AQ. WORM												
CICADAS												
M. CRICKET												
OTHER TERRESTRIALS & ATTRACTORS												

Green River rainbow trout. Jeff Marks photo.

conditions, while the others did not. But even these species are susceptible to future changes in river conditions.

For an aquatic invertebrate to prosper it needs preferred habitat, favorable water temperatures and flows, acceptable substrate conditions and the ability to compete with other aquatic invertebrates for this habitat.

Dams most strongly affect aquatic invertebrates by the timing and duration of both river flows and water temperatures. They alter what would otherwise be natural river flows into controlled release patterns I like to call "regimes." Flow regimes can be defined as patterns of daily or seasonal releases from the dam. Temperature regimes can be defined as how cold or warm the water is for certain periods of time. With both of these regimes, there is often a big difference between what is needed by aquatic invertebrates and what is provided.

One trait of tailwater aquatic insects is that their adult hatches are dense and can occur over weeks, even months. Water temperatures can greatly influence hatch times and their densities. Changes in water temperature are often the result of changes in flow. This may account for the inconsistencies in a hatch's emergence time where flow regimes constantly change. Change the flow regime or temperature and you will change the diversity, density, and emergence patterns of aquatic insects.

Over the years flow regimes on the Green River have been anything but consistent. Hydroelectric power generation, years with drought or flooding, and scientific flows for endangered native fish have contributed to this inconsistency, each having a different flow regime.

Future changes in the pattern of releases from the Flaming Gorge Dam will continue to see some of the Green River's aquatic invertebrates become more dominant, while others could completely disappear, as did many pre-dam species. Consequently, though this chapter reflects today's aquatic invertebrate information, an angler should continue to check in the future for any important changes.

The giant weed beds and spring creek conditions that exist on the Green River today are very conducive to aquatic invertebrate production. An abundance of scuds thrive in this environment and sometimes the midge hatches are astounding in their intensity. Together, because of their large populations, they currently provide the most important dietary food sources for trout. Mayflies and caddis are also present in significantly large enough numbers to be considered important. One Green River study found that 75 percent of a trout's diet consisted of the aquatic invertebrates mentioned above.

It is this huge biomass of aquatic invertebrates that contributes to the Green's ability to sustain large, healthy adult trout populations while still producing incredible growth rates for younger trout. During the growing season, young trout can grow an average of 1.2 inches a month. Trout, young and old, definitely take advantage of the large numbers of these invertebrates in the drift.

Terrestrials, in their season, are also a significant part of the Green River trout's diet. During periods with good aquatic hatches, they supply trout with a supplemental diet. In non-hatch periods, they become the main food source. The importance of these insects in successfully fishing the Green River is often underestimated by anglers.

For some aquatic invertebrate identification I relied on the Flaming Gorge Tailwater Fisheries Investigations' "Factors Influencing Trout Populations and Habitat Utilization, 1987-1989." This study was conducted by the Utah Division of Wildlife Resources.

Cuttbow. *Emmett Heath photo.*

Aquatic Invertebrates

Blue-wing Olives

Ephemeroptera; Baetidae; *Baetis tricaudatus*
Spring: Late March to mid-May
Fall: September to mid-October

Unlike some aquatic insects, *Baetis* mayflies can have more than one hatch annually. On the Green River the strongest hatch occurs in the spring with a secondary one in fall. When the right conditions exist, there is occasionally a *Baetis* hatch during winter. This insect's hatches are best on days that are cloudy, overcast, or even snowy. Sunny days can produce some hatches, but more often it will suppress their numbers and duration.

A blanket hatch of *Baetis* can be a nightmare for anglers. It brings an abundance of trout to the surface, but the huge number of insects combined with selectivity of these trout makes it nearly impossible to have your fly taken.

Baetis hatches usually occur mid-morning to early afternoon, and are often preceded by prolific hatches of midges. While the nymphs live in quiet pools and slow eddies, they are strong swimmers and can be found in heavy strong waters before hatching. Trout may often be observed flashing as they actively pursue emergers at different levels in the river, even in the heaviest of currents. Try suspending your *Baetis* nymph at the trout's level for maximum effectiveness. *Baetis* are best imitated by simple mayfly nymph and low-riding adult patterns with dark olive to gray bodies.

The early spring *Baetis* are the largest adults, size 16 to 18, possibly due to their extended growth period as nymphs overwinter. As the hatches proceed through the season the duns become smaller. Then, size 18 to 20 imitations are most effective.

It is possible there are several sub-species of *Baetis* in the Green River. This may account for the smaller 22 to 24 size *Baetis* that is often present in the fall. Over the years we may have incorrectly referred to these as *Pseudos* (*Pseudocloeon*). Since we have little scientific information that this smaller version is indeed a different species, we will refer to all of them as *Baetis*. For the angler it is important to treat fishing all *Baetis* patterns the same except for their size.

Pale Morning Duns

Ephemeroptera; *Ephemerella inermis*
Mid- to late June to August

Pale morning duns are some of the most widely distributed mayflies in the West. The most common species encountered on the Green River is *inermis*. Their presence brightens up what would otherwise be a long hatchless summer. They will emerge in the sunshine, but usually prefer cool, cloudy days and all types of water. While this mayfly is found from the dam to Browns Park, its numbers are strongest downstream of Little Hole.

The nymphs are classified as sprawlers and prefer rocky or gravelly bottoms with good aquatic vegetation. On the Green River they also seem to adapt well to the silty, sandier types of habitat as well.

Nymphs are darker than the adults, ranging from a mottled tan to deep olive-brown. Their color usually reflects their habitat.

Prior to hatches, effective nymph fishing should be done near the bottom. During emergence the nymphs are very active, but are very slow to emerge from their shucks once on the surface. Because of this try drifting a floating PMD nymph imitation directly to an individual trout early in the hatch.

Adult females are pale yellow while the males are usually a rusty color. The adult stage is best fished with low-profile fly patterns. Trout can be extremely selective to this hatch, even preferring to pick up crippled or failed duns. This can cause much frustration for the angler, but once solved can be turned into an advantage. Their emergence occurs mid-morning around 10:00 a.m. to 11:00 a.m., they then mate, lay eggs, and die the day after emergence.

The spinner fall normally occurs between late evening and early morning. However, I have seen a spinner fall in early afternoon. The spinner females are pale yellow, while the males are rusty in color. The largest pale morning duns, sizes 14 to 16, hatch earliest and as the season goes on, they then tend to be smaller, size 16 or 18. During normal seasonal and water conditions, emergence dates are mid-June through August. However, higher river flows are capable of delaying its start.

Tricos

Ephemeroptera; Tricorythidae; *Tricorythodes*
Late August-October

The appearance of this Green River mayfly hatch has been inconsistent at best. However, in some years it does

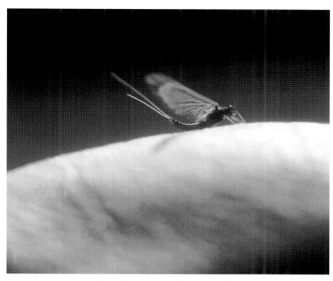

Trico *dun. Larry Castruita photo.*

appear in some numbers, therefore deserving at least an honorable mention. Their appearance coincides with the cooling air and water temperatures going into fall.

The boat ramps at Little Hole are where I usually first notice this hatch. In the early morning sunlight, columns of Trico males can be spotted spiraling into the air. This hatch seldom goes very far upstream from Little Hole, though they can range far downstream, even into the "C" Section. Keep in the mind this is a hatch of short duration. Emergence, mating and the spinner fall can occur within a few short hours. The spinner fall is what most anglers are most familiar with. Usually it is over by 10:30 to 11:00 a.m. Black and white spinner patterns size 20 and smaller are used to match this phase. Small flies and tippet, along with a precise delicate presentation is the best approach to successfully fishing this hatch.

Diptera

Diptera: Chironomidae (midges)
Larvae: All season
Pupae and Adults: Fall, winter, early spring
Diptera: *Simulium* (aquatic black flies)
Larvae: All seasons
Pupae and Adults: April to September

Diptera are undoubtedly the most prolific of all the Green River's aquatic insects. Masses of their spent casings will be found along the river's edge, sometimes measuring ten inches wide, two inches thick, and running for yards. These masses are usually found after the river recedes from a fluctuating flow leaving them along the river's edge.

According to the river studies*, the two most prevalent Diptera taxon, and major trout food sources, are Chironomidae (midges), and *Simulium* (black flies). Chironomids are probably the midge most anglers are familiar with. There were four more taxon mentioned in the study*; Sciomyzidae (marsh flies), Stratiomyidae

(aquatic soldier flies), *Limnophora* (aquatic muscids), and Tipulidae (craneflies). Except for Tipulidae which will be discussed later, we will treat all Diptera as a group.

The minor differences between taxon will not make a great deal of difference to anglers trying to fish these insects. Their life cycle consists of a larva, pupa and adult. As a larva they live in the aquatic vegetation or inhabit some of the sandier areas of the river. In the case of Simulium, the larvae attach themselves to the rocks. These larvae often become dislodged during periods of fluctuating water levels. At other times they can be available to the trout when individuals are active.

The pupal stage of the life cycle is important to the angler. Trout actively feed on or just below the surface by seining in these emerging insects. Their behavior is typified by the bulging surface disturbance or by their noses just barely protruding the water's surface.

Pupal imitations can be fished by floating or suspending them in the film. It is important that the pupae are oriented as the naturals are in the film with their abdomens hanging vertically below the water's surface. Cul-de-canard style or midge patterns with extended poly wing cases are great at accomplishing this.

The adult stage is also a good opportunity for the angler. While individual adult patterns will produce strikes, trout often prefer the clumped midge patterns, such as the Griffith's Gnat. Many anglers are reluctant to fish midges because of their small size. A simple solution

Masses of midge shucks can be found along the river's edges after a large hatch.

to this is what I call "area fishing." After presenting the fly I try to approximate its location. Then imagining its drift, I set the hook on any rise within a several foot radius of that area. This works exceptionally well and you do not even need to see the fly.

Diptera come in a wide variety of colors including: black, olive, gray, brown, tan, red, blood red, and cream. Effective pattern variations are endless. The number one larval pattern is the Brassie in copper, red, green. For the adult use a Griffith's Gnat. Effective imitation sizes range from 16 to 24, with 18 to 22 being the most useful.

Craneflies

Diptera; Tipulidae; *Tipula*
Larvae: Available all year
Adults: Mid-June to August

These giants of the midge family are commonly found in the Green River. Their larva is often called a "rockworm" and is found in several colors ranging from a dirty gray to dirty tan. In the early season they are smaller, sizes 14 to 10, 3X long hook, than just before emergence periods, sizes 10 to 8, 3X long hook, in summer. The larvae become most available during periods of high water when they become dislodged. The adults are most active during the darkness of night. Their activity is usually over early in the morning before most anglers reach the stream. Still, the adult patterns can be fished as an attractor, mimicking the egg-laying adult as it skitters across the water's surface in the early morning hours. A Double Ugly in reddish brown to tan in color also works well. These are tied large, size 10 to 8, 3X or 4X long hooks. The adult at rest resembles a giant mosquito.

Scuds

Crustaceans; Amphipoda; *Gammarus lacustris*
(Freshwater Olive Scud)
Crustaceans; Amphipoda; *Hyalella azteca* (Tiny Olive Scud)
All season

In the Green River, scuds are available to the trout on a year-round basis. Two species exist, the larger *Gammarus lacustris*, and the micro sized *Hyalella azteca*. Both species' preferred habitat is the aquatic vegetation that forms on the river's flowing weed beds or covers its rocky bottom. Pick up a handful of moss and you will find an abundance of these crustaceans. They are very active crawlers and swimmers, but can be caught by trout during periods of activity. When they are inactive, trout can sometimes be seen actively rooting and trying to dislodge them from the weed beds.

In the early morning hours, rocks along the shallow river's edges are active with feeding trout pursuing *Hyalella* scuds. With the frenzy that trout exhibit in this activity, there can be no doubt that these tiny scuds are a preferred food source.

Scud populations are strong because as a species they are prolific in their ability to regenerate. They are also overachievers in competeing with other aquatic invertebrates for their preferred habitat. Color and size can differ within both species, even within the same area, but most will be olive-grayish in color.

When tying imitations to match the natural, I prefer to use Ligas Ultra Translucent Dubbing Material #42 Sparkle Olive Scud with a little gray blended in.

Scuds periodically undergo stages of metamorphic molting, this may result in lighter colors ranging from tan to orangeish pink. The pinkish hues appear most often after scuds have dried on rocks after being stranded by a decreasing river flow. They become available to trout

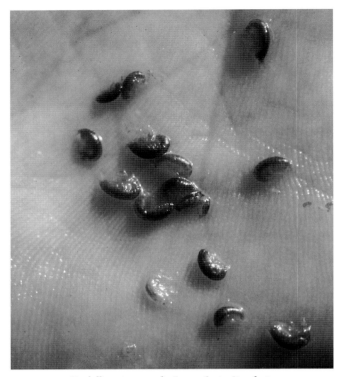

Hyalella azteca *scuds. Larry Castruita photo*

when the river is raised once again. Other successful scud pattern colors are tan, dirty yellow, pink, orange, amber and gray.

Scud imitation sizes can run the full range. *Gammarus* are the largest species, size 14 to 18, while *Hyalella* are almost a micro-scud, size 18 to 24. The common wisdom is to match the natural's actual size by fishing size 14 to 18 or smaller scud patterns. I often go against that approach, especially for float-fishing, preferring instead to use much larger sized scuds. My success rate is high, probably because size 8 to 12 scud patterns also resemble other aquatic foods. Crane flies and caddis larvae are just a couple of examples. Additionally, these larger imitations have useful attractor qualities that many anglers tend to overlook.

Caddis

Micro Caddis
Trichoptera; Hydroptilidae; *Hydroptila*
July to September

What first brought my attention to this tiny micro-caddis was its listing as a major trout food source on the Green River. The study* showed these insects in stomach samples from the dam to Little Hole. It is my guess that they are present in the Green River at least to Red Creek, possibly further. They were found during all seasons. They are often hard to distinguish between some species of Diptera.

The larva is free-living for all but the fifth and final instar. During this period they build a silk-purse-like case and stay attached to rocks or similar structure. The most thorough treatment of this insect I found was in *Western*

Cactus art. Jeff Marks photo.

The Green River in winter.

*Young people can enjoy fishing success on the Green River too!
Below: Red Creek Rapids—river-floaters should scout
this rapid before attempting to run it.*

Dry Flies

Floating Mayfly Nymph, Rust   **RSII, Gray**   **Gray Midge**   **Parachute Griffith's Gnat**   **Griffith's Gnat**   **Fuzz Ball**   **Mating Midge**

Callibaetis Thorax   **Gray Sparkle Dun**   **Compara-Dun, Gray**   **Compara-Dun PMD**   **Parachute BWO**   **Parachute PMD**   **Parachute Adams**

Humpy Red   **Humpy Royal**   **Humpy Yellow**   **Royal Wulff**   **Royal Trude**   **Crystal Trude**   **Rio Grande King**

Elk Hair Caddis   **Goddard Caddis, Black**   **CDC Ant, Black**   **CDC Ant, Cinnamon**   **Flying Black Ant**   **Sailor Ant**   **Foam Beetle**

Royal Stimulator   **Yellow Stimulator**   **Orange Stimulator**   **Joe's Hopper**   **Parachute Hopper, Olive**   **Parachute Hopper, Yellow**

Double Humpy, Black   **Double Humpy, Yellow**   **Double Humpy, Orange**   **Double Ugly**   **Parachute Cricket**

Chernobyl Ant   **Cricada Trude 1**   **Cricada Trude 2**   **Crystal Crippler**   **Crystal Mormon Cricket**

Nymphs

WD-40, Black

WD-40, Red

WD-40, Olive

WD-40, Gray

Beadhead Prince Nymph

Flashback Hare's Ear

Pheasant Tail Nymph, Standard

Pheasant Tail Nymph, Flashback

Pheasant Tail Nymph, Beadhead

Biot Nymph, Red

Biot Nymph, Olive

Biot Nymph, Black

Midge Larva, Red

Midge Larva, Green

Red Marabou Nymph

Brassie, Copper

Brassie, Green

Brassie, Red

San Juan Worm, Red

San Juan Worm, Wine

San Juan Worm, Brown

Green River Worm, Red

Green River Worm, Brown

Flashback Scud, Orange

Flashback Scud, Tan

Flashback Scud, Pink

Matt's Fur

Cranefly Larva

Muddler Minnow

Woolly Bugger, Olive/Black

Woolly Bugger, Crystal Black

Woolly Bugger, Ginger

Platte River Special

Zonker, Black/Gold

Zonker, Natural/Gold

Green River brown trout. Jeff Marks photo.

Pipe Creek during spring runoff.

Bald eagles grace the riverside trees in winter.

Mule deer.

Yellowstone cutthroat. Emmett Heath photo.
Right: Float-fishing the giant back-eddie of the Turnaround Pool.

Some stretches of the river are long glides with depths averaging four to eight feet that restrict wading anglers to the river's shores. A boat allows anglers to access the many trout that occupy these deeper river runs.

Successful anglers fishing from a drift boat. Joe Greybush photo.

One of the advantages of early spring fishing is catching beautiful rainbow trout.

The Green River just below Red Creek Rapids. A great view of the lower river from the Red Creek campsite.

The lower river is home to some healthy brown trout.

A 28-inch Green River brown trout. Jeff Marks photo.

Swallow Canyon, nearly impassable by foot. Emmett Heath photo.

Cuttbow. Emmett Heath photo.

One of the many improved campsites found downriver of Little Hole. They commonly have bench seats, fire rings, and a picnic table. Doug Burton photo.

Underwater rainbow trout. Utah Division
of Wildlife Resources photo.

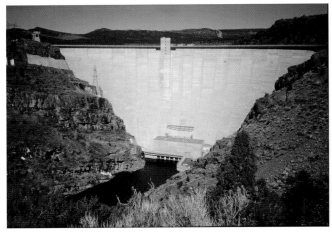

Flaming Gorge Dam.

The large trout population residing in the Green River provides great
opportunities for all anglers. Larry Castruita photo.

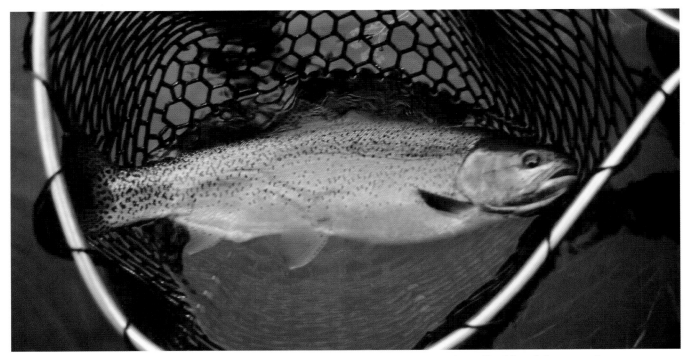

The greatest proof that the "special regulations" work is the presence of large numbers of healthy adult trout, such as
this beautiful rainbow trout, a resource too valuable to be caught only once.

Hatches by Rick Hafele and Dave Hughes. The most important stages of this insect for the angler are probably the larva and pupa.

Small Brassies or simple midge nymph patterns in cream, gray or olive with peacock herl at the head, will effectively imitate the larva. Small soft hackles in sizes 20 to 24 in gray, yellow, brown, orange, and hare's ear should be the most effective pupa imitation.

Most hatches probably go unnoticed because of this insect's minute size. Adults range from 1/16 to 1/4 inch in length, making them very hard to imitate. They emerge mostly in the summer, July, August and September.

Green Rock Worm

Trichoptera; Rhyacophilidae; *Rhyacophila*
July to August

In studies* conducted on the Green River these caddis showed a strong presence in the trout stomach samples. However, they did not rank as a major component of the trout diet. These caddis are free-living in their larval stage, moving about freely on the river bottom. They often lose their grip, making them available as trout food in the current's drift. They prefer the rocky, highly oxygenated fast water river sections. Prime water for these caddis is from Skinny Dip rapids through the Rock Garden to Caddis Wall. Other similar river sections will contain these insects.

The larva and pupa bodies are size 10 to 16, colors range from tan to bright green. The adults range in body color from dark tan to olive, with wings of mottled gray and brown. Emergence of the adults generally occurs in the late afternoon. The egg-laying females fly back to the river in the evening. Twilight can be a productive time for imitations of this caddis species.

The Other Caddis'

Trichoptera; Hydropsychidae; *Hydropsyche*; Spotted Sedge

There are several other species of caddis worthy of note on the Green River. The spotted sedge *Hydropsyche* is also found in the same habitat and has similar emergence periods (July to August) as *Rhyacophila*. They are net spinners and build crude shelters to live in during their larval and pupal stages. They are similar in coloration and size to *Rhyacophila*.

Trichoptera; Brachycentridae; *Brachycentrus*; American *Grannom*

The American *Grannom* caddis, *Brachycentrus*, is a tube-case maker existing in small numbers in the Green River. They emerge in July and August along with other species of caddis. The larva is cased, the pupa is tan to dark brown in sizes 12 to 16. Adults have light tan to brown bodies, gray wings with brown markings and range in sizes 10 to 14.

Trichoptera; Limnephilidae; *Hesperophylax*; Silver Striped Sedge

The largest Green River caddis is the silver stripe sedge *Hesperophylax*. These are commonly known as fall or October caddis. The adults can be as large as a size 6, or even larger. They build cases of rocks, sand, twigs, and other materials. The pupa have a wide variety in body color from brown, tan, green, and yellow.

The adults hatch in July and can remain until they lay eggs in early September. Body color ranges from yellow, orange to amber. An appropriately sized and colored Elk or Bucktail Caddis pattern will suffice in imitating this insect.

Heaven's Gates—the beginning of the "lower river" just below Red Creek Rapids. Doug Burton photo.

This species was found in the largest numbers in trout stomachs near the dam. However, these caddis are found flying around our camp lanterns at night on lower portions of the river. This suggests a much wider distribution than shown in the studies.*

Trichoptera; Limnephilidae; *Psychoglypha*; Snow Sedge

*Flaming Gorge Tailwater Fisheries Investigations' "Factors Influencing Trout Populations and Habitat Utilization, 1987-1989." Utah Division of Wildlife Resources.

The snow sedge is present along the Green River as an adult in February and March. The adults are often found in snowbanks along the river, hence their name. Their cased larvae are active in the daytime and the pupae become active on warm sunny winter days.

These are large caddis, usually found in size 10 to 8. The larva case is dark in color with the larva and pupa being brown. The adult wing is reddish brown with a long silver streak running down the middle. The body is light to dark brown. It is best imitated by using an size 10 Goddard Caddis. This caddis can provide early season dry-fly fishing for the observant angler.

Spring Black Stones

Plecoptera; Taeniopterygidae; *Oemopteryx*
Late March to April

I usually encounter these small stoneflies several times each spring between late March and the end of April. They remind me of a flying ant hatch. In fact I use a small size 14 to 16 Black Flying Ant pattern to imitate the adult stage. The best nymph pattern is a size 14 to 16 Prince Nymph fished at the river's edge just prior to the hatch.

You have to be very observant to even notice this hatch. It usually announces itself with fish noisily feeding on these small stones as they flutter on the river's surface. These are female stones, floating in midstream to lay their eggs on a flat below a riffle. Emergence usually occurs mid- to late in the day. I find these stones in small numbers from Roller Coaster rapid to Diving Board rapid. This is early season fun, but you need to be observant.

Medium Brown Stone (Goldens)

Plecoptera; Perlidae; *Hesperoperla pacifica*
Late June to mid-August

The golden stonefly is not widely distributed in the Green River. Their numbers appear to be strongest in the "B" Section, especially around Washboard rapid. However, I have seen them in the Little Hole area as well as other places.

Emergence periods coincide with other stonefly species, from late June to mid-August. The nymphs are one and a half inches long, yellowish olive in color with brown mottling. Adults are olive to golden. Though this is not a very large hatch, it never hurts to keep a few golden stonefly patterns in your fly box.

Aquatic Worms

Annelida; Oligochaeta
All season

This aquatic earthworm was found in good numbers during the river studies*. Its size is generally two to two and a half inches in length, 3/16 inch in diameter. They are red to reddish brown in color and prefer silty, sandy environments.

Trout can often be seen cruising the sandier beach river areas picking up midge larvae and occasionally worms. We call fish involved in this activity "sand sharks."

The water in these areas tends to be shallow, so when the trout feeds there parts of their fin and tail are exposed giving them a shark-like appearance.

Patterns imitating these aquatic worms can be fished at any time. However, they are most effective when the river is rising or during sustained periods of high water. The San Juan Worm is probably the most well-known fly pattern for this aquatic worm. Many versions exist, many are made from ultra chenille in sizes 10 to 18. In addition to the standard red, other productive colors are wine, brown, and claret.

Terrestrials

Ants

Hymenoptera
April to October

Much has already been written on the love trout have for these small insects. Green River trout are no exception. Because so much is already known about this terrestrial's life cycle, I will go straight to making recommendations.

These are the earliest terrestrials available to trout. they appear in the spring as soon as the snow leaves and are present until the snow flies in November. Their imitations can be effectively fished on all types of water and under varying conditions. They catch trout in the middle of a hatch or put the spark in a slow summer day. Ant patterns are unquestionably one of the most consistently producing surface flies for the Green River.

Along the river's edge you will find a variety in ant color and size. However, the most common ant patterns are black-bodied in sizes 14 to 18. Small red ant imitations can also be useful in sizes 16 to 18, though I have yet to find the perfect fly pattern for them.

Flying ants hatch below Little Hole at different times of the year (May to September). Any flying ant fly pattern that resembles the natural will work well. They are size 14 to 16, black bodied, and have rusty-brown, clear wings.

Most ant fly patterns work on the Green River so bring your favorites. The biggest problem with fishing ant patterns is poor visibility due to their size and color. One remedy is to fish ants as a trailer from a large attractor fly. However, there is one other effective solution to visibility. See "Sailor Ant" in the "Specialty Fly Patterns of the Green River" chapter (page 70).

Beetles

Coleoptera
May to October

Like ants, beetles are usually found along the Green River corridor. They come in a variety of species and sizes including two aquatic versions identified in the river studies*. The aquatic versions are crawling water beetles (Coleoptera; Haliplidae) and riffle beetles (Coleoptera; Optioservus) which showed up in stomach samples taken in summer and fall in the Little Hole area. The quantities were so small as to make imitating them insignificant.

Species found among the ground beetles include the

pine pitch borer, spotted tiger, and stag beetles. This list is not conclusive but represents some of the most common beetles found along the river. They range in color from black, slate gray, metallic green-blue, brown to orangeish brown, according to species.

Beetles start appearing in May, possibly even earlier during dry springs. Effective patterns are black, tied in various sizes and shapes. Usually they are short and round, or long and skinny. Tie imitations with many different profiles. See "Specialty Fly Patterns of the Green River" chapter (pages 73, 73) for two specific patterns; the Foam Beetle and Chernobyl Ant. Small beetles should be size 14 to 16 while the larger ones are size 10 to 12, regular shank and larger.

These patterns should be fished along the river's edge and in its small back-eddies where the naturals are available. They are effectively fished in the river's large back-eddies or wherever trout are milling around or feeding.

Cicadas (Locusts)

Homoptera; Cicadellidae; *Platypedia* ; May to June
Homoptera; Cicadellidae; *Okanagana magnifica*; June to July

Both species are cousins to the 13- and 17-year locusts found in other parts of the United States.

Mention cicadas to a Green River angler who has fished this hatch and you will likely see his eyes get big and excited. Before 1988, anglers were virtually unaware of this insect's presence and the trout's more than casual interest in them. Since their discovery, their imitations have accounted for some unbelievable fishing on the Green River.

The largest problem with cicadas is that creating patterns of the natural's emergence is not an easy endeavor. Individuals require anywhere from three to five years (*Platypedis*) to 13 years (*Okanagana*) underground as nymphs, so predicting their adult cycles has proved difficult.

Platypedias seems to have yearly broods with smaller

Cicadas can often be found in the trees along the river's banks.

Both species of cicada side by side. The largest is
Okanagana, *the smallest is* Platypedia.

hatches for several years leading to a cyclical peak with huge numbers. Following the peak years, hatches are often less than spectacular, even nonexistent. The best cicada hatches seem to occur in years when we experience an early, dry spring. In 1989 my notes show that the first cicadas appeared in the last week of April, but this was unusually early.

Generally numbers are small until mid-May when there are usually sufficient numbers of naturals around to indicate a hatch's strength. To anticipate a trip for fishing the "cicada hatch," look after May 10, with most hatches peaking by mid-June.

The adult's life cycle is about 30 days, but individuals overlap each other's emergence. The trout must have a great memory for these insects because cicada patterns will work long after the hatch is over.

In May of 1990, I sent samples of cicadas gathered along the Green River to Brigham Young University for identification. This was kindly done by Dr. M. W. Nelson, Ph.D. and the following are some excerpts from his letter of June 13, 1990, "I have made a tentative identification to genus: *Platypedia*. The group is common in Utah and elsewhere and there are many known species.

"These insects are sometimes called "locusts." They belong to the same family (Cicadellidae) as their cousins, the 13-year and 17-year locusts common in eastern U.S. The more common usage is cicadas.

"Your specimens measured 19-22 mm. in length from apex of head to apex of wings and from 11-13 mm. in length from apex of head to apex of abdomen.

"The adults feed very little and do no damage except when ovipositioning (ovipositing) their eggs in twigs and stems of trees and shrubs. After the eggs hatch, the young nymphs drop to the ground and dig their entry holes in the soil until they reach the roots of plants where they feed for long periods—some species up to 17 years. After going through several molts (all underground) the nymphs emerged from the ground and crawl up trunks of plants where they cast off the last nymphal skin and become adults. The sounds*** produced by these insects

A medium-sized Mormon cricket natural.

are mating calls after which they mate and lay eggs to repeat the cycle.

"Emergences of nymphs and adults occur in spring in the Northern Hemisphere. I am not aware of emergence occurring in the fall. They are particularly active during warm days at 50 degrees F and above. Below this temperature, they are most easily collected by sweeping juniper ** trees with a bug net."

Adult cicadas have large black wedge-shaped bodies with orange to yellow legs and body highlight markings. Wings are transparent with black veins. The wing's lower edges have orange to yellow outlines. At rest, their wings fold tent-like over their body, similar to caddisflies.

These are clumsy insects when it comes to flying which accounts for so many getting blown onto the water and becoming trout food. Once on the water they can cause a commotion, but generally they drift silently. I sometimes call this the "phantom hatch" because only small numbers of insects ever reach the water. Usually the water number increases on hot days with warm gusts through the river corridor.

Platypedia's hatch has its strongest presence in the "A" Section, but they are found all along the river corridor. The larger *Okanagana* is usually found in the juniper and pinion pines on the bench above Red Canyon. However, once these trees drop in elevation near Little Hole, this cicada species is found along the river all the way into Browns Park. We have collected a few of these cicadas, most are two to two and a half inches in length. A few 13-year cicadas are usually found each year; the last major hatch was in 1995.

** Dr. Nelson refers to juniper trees, but many of my samples also came from the branches of green leafed (deciduous) trees along the river.

*** refers to the male clicking sound, produced by vibrations in his body. As a group they make a monotonous chorus of zzzz or buzzzz!

See "Specialty Fly Patterns of the Green River" (page 70) for effective patterns.

Crickets

Orthoptera; May to October

Field crickets are found in large numbers along the Green River. They become an additional food source for trout after a hard rain or when the river suddenly rises, putting naturals on the water. They are black to brownish black in color. Effective imitations range from a small version, size 14, to a larger size 10, 3X hook. Because of their color, adding a colorful indicator to the fly pattern will improve its visibility on the water. They are great when fishing is slow,or as a searching pattern. See "Specialty Fly Patterns of the Green River" (page 72) for the Parachute Cricket.

Mormon Crickets

Orthoptera; Decticinae; *Nabrus simplax*; June to October

Mormon crickets are only an occasional visitor to the Green River. Masses of these migrating insects develop in the open sagebrush-grassland areas north and south of the river corridor. They are not a true cricket, but in reality a wingless long-horned grasshopper. Their common name comes because they threatened crops of Mormon settlers near Salt Lake City in 1848. Large flocks of seagulls appeared and saved the crops from the invading crickets.

They create one generation annually and go through a series of instars before becoming adults in 60 to 90 days. The crickets travel in migrating "bands" and can travel up to one mile daily on sunny days.

When their path intercepts the Green River, the excitement begins for anglers. As an adult these insects are as large as your thumb. That is quite a morsel for any trout. Mormon crickets are normally black or reddish brown or both. Their numbers are generally so large they actually push each other into the river, and soon blanket the water.

Mormon crickets will often push each other into the water.

Where these insects intersect the river and where they travel afterwards is important to the angler because eggs are laid all along their migration path.

Encounters with these insects have mostly occurred below Little Hole and in the Browns Park area. Trout will quickly satiate themselves when large numbers of these large insects are available. However, as the numbers decrease, trout will get very aggressive for the crickets that remain. This is the best time to present them with large imitations. I have watched trout physically knock these insects into the water, at times almost beaching themselves to accomplish this.

Even when these insects are no longer present, the trout's memory imprint is strong as they continue to eat Mormon cricket patterns. See "Specialty Fly Patterns of the Green River" (page 71) for one of many Mormon cricket patterns. If you fish the Green River in the warmer months, put a few of these flies in your fly box and hope for "crickets."

Large trout love Mormon Crickets!

Mormon crickets set adrift on the river's surface.

Grasshoppers

Orthoptera; May to October

The importance of this insect to Green River trout and anglers parallels any other good trout stream. They provide a large source of protein and are favored by trout anytime they can acquire one. Like ants, much has already been previously written about hoppers and how to fish them, so I will get specific about Green River hoppers. Baby hoppers size 14 to 12, start appearing along the banks of the river in May. Hoppers mature in a short period of time and reach adult size by June. They remain available to the trout until the first good frost of fall.

The Green River hopper species are similar to grasshoppers found anywhere in the west. Green River guide Doug Burton says "hoppers are hoppers, you need big ones and little ones in several different colors to match them all". He is right, and certainly that approach will serve your needs well on this river. However, the trout do seem to have some pattern preferences. Low-profile flies such as Dave's Hopper, Henry's Fork Hopper, or, my favorite, a Parachute Hopper, work best on Green River trout. Size 12 to 10 green-bodied hoppers represent the smaller meadow hoppers. For other species sizes 10 to 6 with cream to tan bodies with mottled wings work well.

In their season, properly fished hoppers are effective anywhere along the Green River.

Other Insects

I have tried to provide a comprehensive look at the major aquatic insects, invertebrates and terrestrials of the Green River. It is impossible to cover every insect in detail. Known exclusions are aquatic snails (*Gyraulus*), damselflies (especially around the large water impoundments in Browns Park). The large speckle-winged mayfly duns that appear on occasion in the silty stretches of the "C" Section are *Callibaetis*.

Specialty Fly Patterns of the Green River

As with most rivers that provide interesting challenges, interesting solutions are often developed. This is especially true of the many specialty patterns developed for the Green River. Many were born from the need to more accurately match the river's insects, others are the product of vivid imaginations. Whatever their origins, the Green River has its own unique fly patterns. Some are what I classify as "guide flies." These are productive patterns developed by guides on the river. Sometimes a pattern's origin comes from exposure to the many flies given to a river guide by guests. Whatever their origin, they are often kept under wraps for several years before obtaining notoriety and being accepted as a standard fly.

Many of them are great cross-over patterns that achieve considerable success on other rivers. This points out that a good fly pattern often works well, but a great fly pattern will work anywhere. What is special about the following patterns is that most are not known outside of the Green River area. Reference the suggested pattern charts at the end of each "Green River Calendar" chapter or consult Appendix D, "Master Fly Pattern Index" (page 77), for other effective fly patterns for the river. Many of the specialty patterns presented are either attractor or terrestrial in nature. This should re-emphasize the importance placed on these types of flies for mid- to late season anglers visiting the Green River.

One basic rule for tying flies for this river is to think "basic black." This color is contained in many of the more productive Green River patterns. The logic behind its success escaped me for some time. However, when you think about it, it makes sense. Midges, stoneflies, caddis, ants, beetles, crickets, grasshoppers and cicadas all contain species with black on some basic part.

A second rule is to think "shiny." From Electric Scuds to Flashback Pheasant Tails, shiny is effective. Do not limit this practice to only nymphs either. Many of the dry-fly patterns are tied with black or peacock crystal chenille.

Sailor Ant

Several years ago at a fly fishing show I met Bill Skilton of Boiling Springs, Pennsylvania. Bill is an innovator with fly-tying materials. His little foam cylinder ant bodies with their white top caught my eye immediately. Since that day I have always kept a good supply of patterns tied with these bodies. We affectionately call them "Sailor Ants" because of their black suits with white caps. They float extremely well, are visible and, most importantly, they are deadly when used on trout.

Bill sells these to the Orvis Company where they are available as Quick Sight Ants, so other anglers must also agree. I have seen them tied in many different styles. Following is my Green River style.

Sailor Ant

Hook: Daiichi 1310, 1X, short.
Size: 12 to 18.
Thread: Danville's black 3/0 or stronger, try other colors for variety. Cover hook with thread before tying body on.
Body: Match body size to hook.
Legs: Try a variety of materials, from a few strands of Krystal Flash to small rubber legs.
Tying Tip: Place indicator portion of cylinder ahead of the hook eye for proportion. After fly is tied, trim the rear portion of the cylinder to size.

Cricada Trude

"Cicada Madness" is what Rex Gerlach called his article featured in the 1993 May issue of *Fly Fisherman* Magazine. I supplied this recipe for the article and it was one of the featured patterns (low profile).

For me, this cicada pattern has now become a fly style, such as a Wulff, where the tying style stays the same, but the different tying materials define the actual fly.

Try wings of elk, deer, or white calf hair. Underwings can range from different colors of Krystal Flash to pearlescent Mylar sheets. Bodies can be plain black foam or covered with various colors of crystal chenille. Rubber legs can be the standard black, but flies with yellow or orange legs are also effective. The addition or absence of each tying material will give the fly a different look altogether.

I have re-named this fly the Cricada Trude. This reflects the fact that this pattern imitates a cricket, cicada, in a Trude format. This fly sits low in the water like many natural insects and it fishes well as an attractor.

Cricada Trude

Hook: Daiichi 1710.
Size: 12 to 6.
Thread: Danville's FlyMaster Plus, black.
Body: Black foam strip, plain or covered with crystal chenille. Cut the foam strip to make it the hook's gap width.
Underbody: Black foam strip when crystal chenille is used.
Underwing: Few strands of Krystal Flash (pearl, rainbow, orange).
Wing: Elk, natural deer hair, calf tail.
Legs: Round rubber hackle (black, yellow, orange).
Indicator: White or yellow foam.
Head: Black foam strip body is extended out front. After wing and legs are tied in, foam is pulled back to form the head. Trim. If desired, the indicator is added to finish the fly.

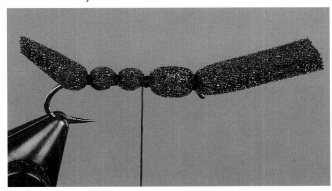

This is what the underbody of the Cricada Trude looks like before adding the other features. Jim Schollmeyer photo.

The finished Cricada Trude. Jim Schollmeyer photo.

Trudes

Rio Grande King Trude (O'Conner)

Before I knew how much trout loved cicadas I always wondered why they went for this fly pattern. It is not only a great imitation of a cicada, but a great attractor as well. Many Green River trout have fallen for this easy-to-see fly.

Its advocate, Dick O'Connor, believed this fly contained the solid basic element and color that make up a great trout fly. I will never forget my visit with him on the South Platte River in Colorado many years ago, and my introduction to this fly. He was well-known for the large trout that fell victim to his favorite fly and loved to fish it wet, and as a dry fly. Smaller sizes are perfect during the hot summer months when trout are sulking or selective. It is also a great indicator fly when fishing a dropper.

Rio Grande King Trude (O'Connor)

Hook: Daiichi 1180.
Size: 14 to 10.
Tail: Golden pheasant tippets.
Tag: Gold tinsel (if desired). Some anglers swear to its necessity!
Body: Black chenille.
Wing: White calf tail.
Hackle: Furnace or coachman brown.

Crystal Trude

Hook: Daiichi 1710.
Size: 10 to 14.
Body: Black crystal chenille.
Note: This version of the Trude is one I developed to give this fly a little more sparkle. The hook shank is longer than the original fly, this allows for a fuller body and longer wing. If it is possible, this version outfishes the original. It is helpful to use a small piece of foam as an underbody on the larger versions.

Crystal Mormon Cricket

There are more Mormon cricket patterns than you can imagine. After several seasons of experimenting, I came up with this one. It has always worked well and floats extremely well for a large fly. Tying crazy flies like this is part of the fun of fishing the Green River, but fishing them is even more fun.

Hook: Daiichi 1710 or 1720.
Size: 4 to 6.
Tail: 3 round rubber legs brown or orange.
Underbody: (Optional) Strip of foam.
Overbody: Long fiber, brown crystal chenille.
Wing and Head: Dyed reddish brown deer hair.
Tying Tip: The cut ends of the deer hair clump are tied in over the fly's body with the natural ends extending one hook shank length beyond the eye of the hook. After the legs are added, this batch of deer hair is then pulled back over the fly and secured to form the head and wing of the fly. The indicator is then added to finish the fly.
Front Legs: Same as tail.
Indicator: Fluorescent orange deer hair or yarn.

Crystal and Peacock Crippler

Former Green River guide Butch Hicks has to be given credit for exposing the Green River trout to this productive pattern. Its buggy nature combined with the movement of the rubber tails often brings action. Try it during the cicada hatch as an effective imitation, or as an attractor

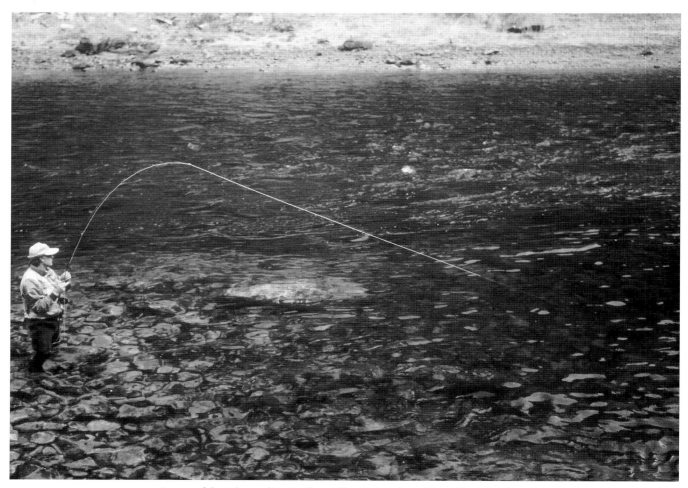

A successful angler wading the Green River at low flows. Larry Castruita photo.

on a slow day. Whether fished on the surface in large pools or the river edges, this fly produces! The original fly had a peacock herl body which I replaced with black crystal chenille, both versions work great!

Crystal and Peacock Crippler
Hook: Daiichi 2220.
Size: 12 to 6.
Thread: Danville's Black Monocord 3/0.
Tail: Three long, round rubber hackle sections, black.
Front and Rear Hackle: Gloss black, dry-fly quality.
Body: Black crystal chenille or peacock herl.
Indicator: Fluorescent yarn or deer hair, yellow or white foam.

Parachute Cricket

This is a simplified cricket pattern that is fast to tie and works well under a number of conditions. Guy Collett at the Flaming Gorge Lodge's fly shop says it is hard to keep these flies on hand. The parachute is essential because black is hard to see on its own on the water. Try smaller sizes throughout the season and larger sizes during cicada time.

Parachute Cricket
Hook: Daiichi 1720.

Size: 8 to 14.
Thread: Danville's Black FlyMaster Plus.
Post: White Poly Yarn.
Hackle: Black.
Rear Body: Black Larva Lace Tying Foam, strip wrapped around hook shank to form body.
Body: Black dubbing under parachute.
Wing: Shimazaki Fly Wing #3 (medium gray).
Legs: Black goose quill sections knotted.
Ovipositor: Black midge Larva Lace.

Chernobyl Ant

This overexposed radiation ant is a great imitator of many terrestrial trout foods found on the Green River. Some are beetles, crickets, and Mormon crickets. Allan Woolley, Mark Forslund and other guides of Western Rivers Flyfisher are the main originators of this outstanding bug.

Many different ties of this fly exist, the most simple pattern is listed here. Different body widths and leg formations are common variations. This is a great pattern, simple but effective.

Chernobyl Ant
Hook: Daiichi 1720 or 2220.
Size: 10 to 4.

Thread: Black FlyMaster Plus.
Body: Black foam strip, one hook gap wide.
Legs: Round black rubber hackle.
Indicator: Yellow foam.

Foam Beetle

Foam beetles are generally more durable than many deer hair beetles. They float well, are easy to tie, and are highly effective. What more could you ask for?

Foam Beetle
Hook: Daiichi 1560.
Size: 18 to 10.
Thread: Danville's Black FlyMaster Plus.
Body: Thin black foam strip.
Legs: Round rubber hackle.
Indicator: Yellow foam strip.

Parachute Griffith's Gnat

Everyone knows the effectiveness of the standard Griffith's Gnat. Sometimes the only problem when using it is visibility. Guy Collett, purveyor of flies for the Flaming Gorge Lodge fly shop, came up with a simple solution to this problem with visibility with his addition of the poly yarn tuft near the head of the fly. While not truly a parachute, the poly yarn indicator gives it the effectiveness that the white post gives a parachute. This variation works very well, try one! Several other top Green River midge patterns that Guy offered are the Fuzzball and Parachute Mating Midge.

Parachute Griffith's Gnat
Hook: Daiichi 1180.
Size: 18 to 22.
Thread: Danville's 6/0 black.
Body: Peacock herl.
Hackle: Grizzly.
Indicator: White poly yarn.

Fuzzball
Hook: Daiichi 1180.
Size: 20 to 22.
Thread: Danville's 6/0 black.
Tail: Grizzly and brown hackle fibers mixed.
Body: Grizzly and brown hackle mixed.

Parachute Mating Midge
Hook: Daiichi 1180.
Size: 18 to 22.
Thread: Danville's 6/0
Body: Black thread.
Hackle: Grizzly, sparse fore and aft.
Indicator: White poly yarn.

Cranefly Larvae

I have used several different cranefly larva patterns in the past but this one has worked best for me. Try not to overbuild the bodies, keep them thinner and elongated.
Hook: Daiichi 2220 bent down on front third. The pre-bent

hooks offered by other hook manufacturers are nice, but most have very large diameter hook wire that I believe can damage the trout.
Size: 12 to 6.
Body: Tan and brown variegated chenille.
Overdubbing: #38 Cream Fox Ligas Ultra Translucent Dubbing Material.
Head: Dubbed dark brown fur.
Rib: Gold wire.
Weighted: Small lead wire to keep body profile small.

Flashback Scud

There seems to be a proliferation of flashy nymph patterns these days. With all of the new synthetic fly-tying materials available, possible combinations are endless and many are extremely effective. I have provided several color variations on the Flashback Scud that have performed well on the Green River. Other body colors could also be substituted.

Tan Flashback Scud (Sometimes known as the 19.5 Scud)
Hook: Daiichi 1130.
Size: 10 to 16.
Thread: Danville's olive or brown 3/0.
Tail: Wood duck dyed mallard, or none.
Rib: Gold or copper wire.
Shellback: Pearlescent Mylar sheet cut in strips.
Body: Dubbed Ligas Ultra Translucent Dubbing Material #19 sand and #20 dirty yellow mixed equally.
Note: Weight when used for float-fishing.

Pink Flashback Scud
Tail: Plain or pink dyed mallard, or none.
Thread: Danville's 3/0 in color complementary to body.
Body: Fly-Rite Polyseal #1, fluorescent pink chopped, mixed and dubbed.

Additional Patterns

WD40 (*Baetis* imitation with San Juan River origins)
Hook: Daiichi 1130.
Size: 16 to 22.
Thread: Olive Danville's 6/0 waxed.
Tail: Wood duck dyed mallard.
Body: Shaped by thread.
Wingcase: Wood duck dyed mallard.
Thorax: Dubbed muskrat.
Other Versions: Red, black, gray.

Double Ugly (attractor)
Hook: Daiichi 1720.
Size: 10 to 6.
Thread: Black monocord 3/0.
Rear Hackle: Grizzly.
Middle Hackle: Reddish brown.
Front Hackle: Grizzly.
Body: Peacock herl between hackles.

Appendix A

Green River Fishing Regulations

The Green River is under special regulations established in 1985.
Trout limits: Licensed anglers, three trout—two under 13 inches and one over 20 inches. Unlicensed anglers 13 years of age or younger, two trout—two under 13 inches or one under 13 inches and one over 20 inches. All trout between 13 inches and 20 inches must be released immediately. Once the limit is reached, fishing must cease.
Fishing by: Artificial lures and flies only. (no scents/attractants)
Season: Year-round.
Refer to current fishing proclamation for any changes.

Note: The practice known as the "San Juan Shuffle" is prohibited on the Green River under the definition and restrictions of "chumming." Chumming is defined as; dislodging or depositing in the water any substance not attached to a hook, line or trap, which may attract fish!

One factor helping to establish the Green River as a world-class fishery came in 1985 in the form of special (quality) regulations. Data collected from studies conducted from 1978 to 1981 by the Utah Division of Wildlife Resources biologists revealed some interesting facts. According to the data, young and old trout are the most likely to die from natural causes. Few fish survived the first year or reached 14 inches in length due to heavy fishing pressure and harvest. Fish planted in April were gone by July.

Further data showed high winter mortality rates due to poor winter habitat for young trout. Annually more than 33,000 fish died after being caught and released on bait, compared with only 2000 caught on flies and artificial lures. The river was managed for quantity to satisfy the harvest-oriented public's demand for catchable trout. Biologically the trout population could not overcome its problems as fishing pressure increased.

The new regulations, as formulated by UDWR's Green River project biologist Ray Johnson, addressed the biological issues of overfishing, winter loss, and hooking mortality. The 13- to 20-inch slot limit provided protection from overfishing. These regulations require that a substantial proportion of the adult trout caught be released and made available to other anglers. A slot limit instead of catch and release appeased the harvest and trophy-oriented anglers. These 13- to 20-inch fish were capable of surviving winter and more than one season. Artificial fly and lure restrictions helped relieve the hooking mortality rates. Year-round fishing was introduced to alleviate opening day crowding and spread fishing pressure over the entire season. Additionally, the voluntary catch-and-release of harvestable trout has contributed significantly to the overall quality of the Green River trout fishery.

Appendix B

Green River Boating Regulations

- No motors are allowed on boats on the Green River between Flaming Gorge Dam and the Utah/Colorado state lines.
- All boats must carry a spare oar and bailing device, (a small pail will do). Canoes are required to have floatation chambers. Boats 16 feet and over in length must carry a throw bag. All boaters are required to wear life jackets (personal floatation devices) while floating the river. While these are the boating regulations at the time of this printing, be sure to check current regulations before boating the river.
- All Sections: Children 12 years and younger must wear life jackets at all times.

Fishing from a boat provides a great approach to many "bank hugging" trout in the Green River.

• "A" Section: Life jackets must be worn at all times while floating the river. No exceptions.

• "B" Section: Life jackets must be worn at all times while floating the river from Little Hole to Red Creek camp (one-quarter mile below Red Creek Rapids). Life jackets can then be removed to Indian Crossing boat ramp.

• "C" Section: Life jackets must be worn at all times between Indian Crossing boat ramp to 100 yards below Taylor Flats bridge, after which they may be removed.

Typically Coast Guard Approved Type I or Type III PFDs (personal floatation devices) are worn by floaters. For float-fishing, Type III is the most comfortable. Commercial operations are required to use Type I or Type V, these feature a collar flap to keep your head out of the water.

The portions of the Green River where one is allowed to remove the life jacket are described in the regulations as "designated flat water." Of course you may always remove your life jacket when out of the boat. If you are wading you might want to wear it for added safety.

Life jacket violations can result in hefty fines. Boating regulations and enforcement are the responsibility of Ashley National Forest and the Utah Division of Parks and Recreation. Utah has some of the toughest white-water regulations of any western state. The mandatory wearing of life jackets is the one most complained about. On the Green River there have been a number of drownings in the past. For your safety and those who might have to save your life—wear your life jacket! Put your fishing vest on the boat seat back or bench seat to avoid being encumbered by excessive gear.

Appendix C

Floating Etiquette

Some readers may wonder why this subject is important enough to be in a guide book. The truth is, very little has ever been written about how boaters should properly interact with others on any river. In the past, the lack of guidelines has accounted for conflicts between users of navigable rivers. It would be nice if we could all depend on the "golden rule," but without some order chaos often reigns.

This lack of etiquette needs to change, making each day astream more pleasant for all. It is not my intention to dictate rules, but rather provide a way of looking at this subject. Lacking any other established guidelines, this is my best effort based on personal river experiences. At minimum, they reflect how I would like to be treated each day on the river. Please keep in mind, these suggestions do not deal with every possible scenario, not all are predictable.

The Guidelines

Use common sense: Avoid conflicts. Be patient with the inexperienced, even though you know it is rude to crowd others by parking, anchoring, or wading in close proximity to others already utilizing an area. For fly fishermen there has always been a "first one there" right-of-way premise, respect that! One way to visualize this is to think of any water vessel as having a minimal 30-foot radius (the distance of a common cast) around it. Double that, then try to stay well out of it. If you unknowingly crowd

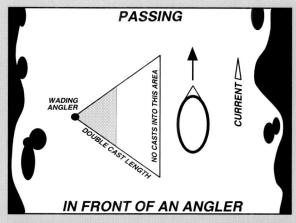

PASSING

IN FRONT OF AN ANGLER

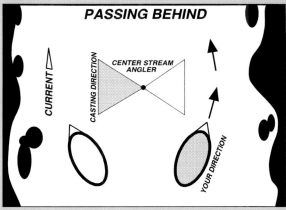

PASSING IN FRONT OF A BOAT

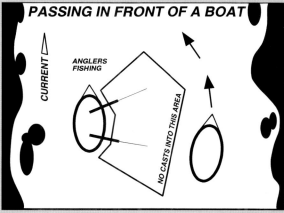

PASSING BEHIND

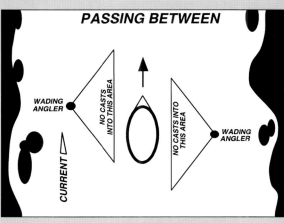

PASSING BETWEEN

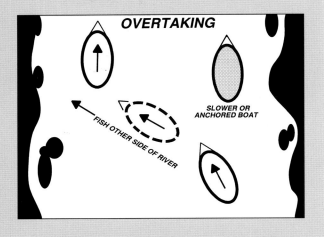

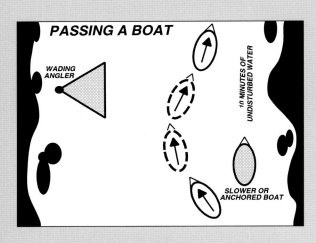

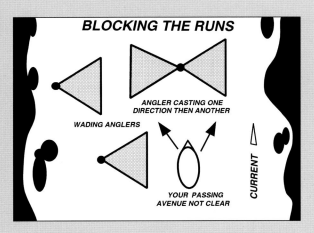

someone, be apologetic, leave as quickly and with as little impact as possible. Let's give each other a break.

Passing in Front: When passing in front of a wading angler or boat, give them as wide a berth as is safely possible. No casts should be made in their direction, completely stop casting if necessary. Try not disturb the water where others are fishing, don't compete for their fish. When passing requires floating over their fishing water, minimize your impact with extreme caution and quiet.

Passing Behind: Pass behind a center stream angler or an anchored boat when there is adequate room and water. This is a judgment call as to whether there is room and where the anglers are fishing. One problem I often encounter is when an angler who is fishing one direction as I approach changes his fishing direction after I have started to pass. It takes a boat some floating distance to make a change in course, once committed to a path, maintain it.

Passing Between: When approaching two boats or wading anglers on both banks, the only reasonable path is directly between. (There is really no option.) This is a tough one because it sometimes requires floating over their water. But remember you did not create the situation.

Overtaking: The first option when overtaking another boat is to fish the other side of the river. Sometimes having to fish a less desirable run forces you to learn a new piece of water, which often results in new discoveries. Trout prefer moving away from constant pressure, they will sometimes be found utilizing somewhat marginal areas.

Passing a Boat: When other boats or bank anglers will not allow using the other side of the river, pass, allowing a minimum of 10 minutes of fresh fishing water for the other boat. Out of sight is even better when possible. It is common for boats to pass. However, it is rare for the passing boat not to pull immediately back in and start fishing in front of the other boat. If you pass a boat, give them a break by giving up a little river before you resume fishing.

Re-entering Traffic: When a boat anchors, approaching moving boats have the right away. The anchored boat should wait until the other traffic has passed then allow several minutes to go by to avoid crowding. Quickly pulling up anchor at the approach of another boat or pulling out in front of another boat is inconsiderate. Look and check the traffic before entering the drift again, just like highway driving.

Changing River Sides: Check for other boats before maneuvering to the other side of the river. It is extremely rude to move clear across the river in front of another boat and start fishing. If you must fish the other side of the river, let the other boats pass first and then move across. This may require waiting or anchoring until clearance and time between boats can be acquired.

Blocking the Runs: Boaters should not drop anchor or park in the middle of a run, especially if it crowds the only safe passage through the area.

Waders: Wading anglers should give clear signals of where they want to fish to boaters. Most experienced boaters will do their best to give waders every courtesy if given some indication of the wader's intent. Boaters who do not are usually inexperienced or do not believe in the golden rule. Waders should not hole-jump floating anglers by racing downstream. Within a few minutes most floaters are past you. Waders should also be aware not to block the only safe passage for boaters.

Appendix D

Master Fly Pattern Index

SCUDS: All season
As Attractors, 8-12
Tan, orange, pink
Gammarus, 14-18
Olive, gray,
Olive-gray, amber
Hyallela azteca, 18-22
Olive, gray,
Olive-gray
Others
Flashback (Electric)
  Scud, 10-18
Pink, 19.5

MIDGES: All season

Larva, Pupa, 16-24
Brassies, copper, red, green
Midge Larva, red, green
Serendipity, red, black, olive
Disco, red, green, pearl,
WD 4, red, black
Biot Midges, red, olive, black
Kimball's Emerger
Kaufmann's Chironomid
Adult Dry, 18 to 24
Black Midge
Olive Midge
Grizzly Midge
Tan Midge
Griffith's Gnat
Parachute Griffith's Gnat
Parachute Mating Midge,
Adams
Parachute Adams

CRANEFLY

Larvae: All season
Adult: July to August
Larva, 6-12
Cranefly Larva
  Tan, olive or gray
Rockworm
Adult, 6-10
Double Ugly

BAETIS

April to mid-May
September to October
Nymphs, 16 to 20
Pheasant Tail
WD40, olive or gray;
RSII, gray or olive
Hare's Ear

Duns, 16 to 22
Parachute Adams
Parachute Blue-wing Olive
Sparkle Dun (Mathews)
  Gray or olive
Compara-dun
  Gray or olive

PALE MORNING DUN

Mid-June
Nymphs, 14 to 18
Pheasant Tail
Floating Mayfly Nymph
Dun, 14 to 18
Parachute PMD
Compara-dun PMD
Sparkle Dun PMD

TRICO

Late August to October
Nymph, 20 to 22
  Tan or brown
Mayfly Nymph
Spinner, 18 to 22
  Black/white
  Polywing Spinner

CALLIBAETIS

September to October
Nymph, 12 to 16
Gold Ribbed Hare's Ear
Pheasant Tail
Dun, 14 to 16
Callibaetis Thorax

MICRO CADDIS

July to September
Larva, Pupa, 20 to 24
Brassie, copper, red, green
Chamois Caddis
Soft Hackles
  Gray, yellow,
  Orange
Adult
Micro Sized Elk
  Hair Caddis

GREEN ROCK WORM

July to August
Larva, Pupa, 10 to 16
Green Latex Worm
Partridge & Green
Soft Hackles
Adult, 12 to 14
Deer Hair Caddis

SPOTTED SEDGE

July to August
Same as "Green Rock Worm"

AMERICAN GRANNOM

July to August
Larva, Pupa, 12 to 16
Zug Bug
Hare's Ear
Chamois Caddis
Yellow Peeking Caddis
Adult, 10 to 14
Deer Hair Caddis, tan

SNOW SEDGE

February to March
Larva, Pupa, 10 to 6
Larva
LaFontaine's
  Dark Cased Caddis
Pupa
LaFontaine's
  Brown Deep Sparkle Pupa
Adult, 10 to 6
Dark Bucktail Caddis
Goddard Caddis

OCTOBER CADDIS

July to September
Larva, Pupa, 12 to 8
Cased caddis
  patterns
Adult, 6 to 10
Bucktail Caddis
  orange, brown

SPRING BLACK STONES

Late March to April
Nymph, 14 to 16
Prince
Adult, 14 to 16
Black Flying Ant
Rio Grande King Trude
Crystal Trude

MEDIUM BROWN
STONE (GOLDEN)

June to mid-August
Nymph, 10 to 8
Rubber Legs
Brown Stone (Anderson)
Golden Stone
Adult
June to mid-August
10 to 6
Stimulator
  Yellow, olive, orange
Golden Stone

AQUATIC WORMS

All season

10 to 16
San Juan Worms
  Red, wine or brown
Green River Worm, red,
  brown

ANTS

April to October
12 to 18
Sailor Ant
Black Fur Ant
Red Ant
CDC Ant
McMurray Ant
Flying Ant

BEETLES

May to October
Foam Beetle
  10 to 16
Chernobyl Ant
  6 to 10
Crowe Beetle
  14 to 18

CICADAS

May to June
10 to 8
Foam Cicada
Cricada Trude
Black Madam X
Black Muddler

CRICKETS

May to October
Parachute Cricket
  8 to 14
Dave's Cricket
  8 to 14
Black Muddler
  8 to 12
Letort Cricket
  8 to 12

MORMON CRICKET

June to October
Crystal Mormon Cricket
  4 to 6

GRASSHOPPERS

May to October

Schroeder's Parachute
6 to 12
Standard Olive
Dave's Hopper
6 to 12
Joe's Hopper
6 to 12
Stimulators
6 to 10
Yellow, orange or olive
Henry's Fork
8 to 10

ATTRACTORS

Royal Wulffs
8 to 18
Humpys
8 to 18
Yellow, black or red
Royal Humpy
8 to 14
Double Humpy
12 to 6
Yellow, fluorescent orange,
red, black
Trudes
10 to 14
Royal Rio Grande King
Crystal

OTHER USEFUL DRY FLIES

Adams
14 to 20
H & L Variant
10 to 14
Light Cahill
14 to 16
Renegade
10 to 20

STREAMERS

2 to 8
Woolly Buggers
Black, black-olive,
ginger, brown, olive,
white
Crystal Buggers
Zonkers
Black/gold
Natural/gold
Muddler Minnows
Dark Spruce Fly
Platte River Specials

Appendix E
Informational Sources and Services

State Agencies

Utah Division of Parks and Recreation
1636 West North Temple
Salt Lake City, UT 84116
(801) 538-7221
(435) 885-3184, Dutch John
Boating and river running
laws and enforcement. State
outfitter registration and professional guides certification.

Utah Division of Wildlife Resources
P.O. Box 158
Dutch John, UT 84023
(435) 885-3164
Flaming Gorge Fisheries
Information.
Contact: Biologists Steve
Brayton or Roger
Schneidervin.

Federal Agencies

Bureau of Land Management, Vernal District
170 South 500 East
Vernal, UT 84078
(435) 789-1362
Manages federal lands and
the lower river within Browns
Park.

Bureau of Land Management John Jarvie Ranch-Historical Site
(435) 885-3307

Bureau of Reclamation
P.O. Box 278
Dutch John, UT 84023
(435) 885-3106
Oversees reservoir storage
and monthly water releases.

U.S. Fish and Wildlife Service
2078 Administration Building
1745 West 1700 South
Salt Lake City, UT 84104
Recovery programs for
endangered, rare native
Colorado fishes.

U.S. Forest Service

Flaming Gorge National Recreation Area Ranger District Headquarters
P.O. Box 278
Manila, UT 84046
(435) 784-3445
Manages reservoir and
national recreation area.

U.S. Forest Service
Ashley National Forest
P.O. Box 157
Dutch John, UT 84023
Manages river corridor and
guide services.

Western Area Power Administration
257 East 200 South, Suite 475
Salt Lake City, UT 84111
Markets electricity produced
and controls hourly water
releases from the dam.

Lodging

Flaming Gorge Lodge
Dutch John, UT 84023
(435) 889-3773
Lodging, dining, convenience
store with tackle shop, full-
service gas station, raft
rentals and shuttles.

Red Canyon Lodge
790 Red Canyon Road
Dutch John, UT 84023
(435) 889-3759
Mark Wilson
Lodging, dining, convenience
store with tackle shop, private lake, High Uinta hunting
and fishing, and horse rides.

Spring Creek Ranch
Guest Ranch
P.O. Box 284
Dutch John, UT 84023
(307) 350-3005

Associations

Flaming Gorge Natural History Association
P.O. Box 188
Dutch John, UT 84023
(435) 885-3305
Local source for river maps,
books and publications.

Green River Outfitters and Guides Association (GROGA)
P.O. Box 416

Dutch John, UT 84023
Represents guides and outfitter companies, providing services on the Green River.

Fishing Guides and Outfitters

Ashley National Forest Permitees
Provide full-service, guided,
walk/wade fishing, float-fishing, scenic trips, and information. (For the river only)

Eagle Outdoor Sports
Rex Mumford
1507 S. Haight Creek
Kaysville, UT 84037
(801) 451-7436
Fishing and scenic trips. Boy
scout and church groups.

Flaming Gorge Lodge
U.S. Hwy. 191
Dutch John, UT 84023
(435) 889-3773 or 889-3783
Fishing and scenic trips,
shuttles, raft rentals, tackle
shop.

Flaming Gorge Recreation Services
P.O. Box 367
Dutch John, UT 84023
(435) 885-3191
Fishing and scenic trips,
shuttles, raft rentals, tackle.

Green River Drifters
Greg Tipton
P.O. Box 773281
Steamboat Springs, CO 80477
(970) 879-0370
Fishing and scenic trips.

Green River Outfitters
Mark Brown
P.O. Box 200
Dutch John, UT 84023
(435) 885-3338 or 781-0434
Fishing and scenic trips, raft
rentals, shuttles, fly shop.

Old Moe Guide Service
Terry Collier
P.O. Box 308
Dutch John, UT 84023
(435) 885-3342
Fishing and scenic trips.

Trout Creek Flies
Dennis and Grace Breer
P.O. Box 247

Dutch John, UT 84023
(435) 885-3355
1-800-835-4551
Fax: (435) 885-3356
Website:
www.fishgreenriver.com
e-mail: dbreer@union-tel.com
Fishing, river camping, and scenic trips.

Western Rivers Flyfisher
Steve Schmidt and
Emmett Heath
865 East 900 South
Salt Lake City, UT 84105
(801) 521-6424
1-800-545-4312
Fishing and scenic trips, Salt Lake City fly shop.

Scenic Outfitter Hatch River Expeditions
Meg Hatch, P.O. Box 1150
Vernal, UT 84078
800-342-8243

Full- and half-day scenic trips. Also whitewater rafting in Utah/Colorado/Idaho.

Nearest Full-service Cities

(Mileages are from the Flaming Gorge Dam)

Salt Lake City, UT: 208 miles; Major airline connection and car rentals.

Rock Springs, WY; 71 miles; local airport with daily commercial airline services and car rentals.

Green River, WY: 73 miles
Manila, UT: 34 miles
Vernal, UT: 42 miles; local airport with daily commercial airline services and car rentals.

Dutch John and the Flaming Gorge National Recreation Area
Dutch John, UT: 2 miles; has limited services.

Local Services
Flaming Gorge Recreational Services:
Convenience store with tackle shop and snack bar, service station with gas, auto repairs, raft rentals, shuttles, showers, and storage yard. (435) 885-3191.

Green River Outfitters
Convenience store with fly shop, raft rentals, shuttles, showers, laundromat.
435-885-3338
U.S. Hwy. 191 and Little Hole Road, Dutch John, UT

Dutch John Airport
Airstrip: 6800 feet, paved.
Services: Aircraft tie downs.
(435) 885-3338.

Flaming Gorge National Recreation Area
(435) 784-3445 or 885-3135
Reservoir, marinas, campgrounds, Green River.
Campground reservations
1-877-444-6777
No campsites with electricity are available, most have water and some have dumping stations. Many are hosted.

U.S. Post Office
Dutch John, UT 84023

Index